THE EIGHT ELEMENTS
My Journey Through Life's Mysteries

Ranchor Prime is the author of ten previous books, including *Birth of Kirtan, When the Sun Shines* and *Hinduism and Ecology.* His book *Bhagavad Gita: Talks Between the Soul and God* led to the inspiration for *The Eight Elements.*

D1738755

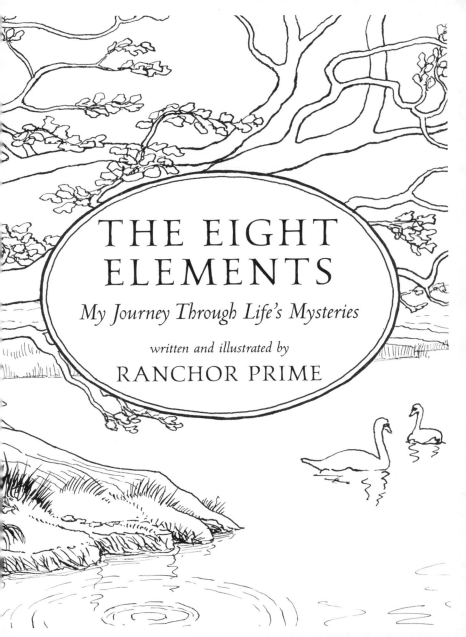

THE EIGHT ELEMENTS

ELEMENTS

My Journey Through Life's Mysteries

written and illustrated by

RANCHOR PRIME

Published by Fitzrovia Press 2017
text and illustrations copyright © Ranchor Prime 2017

Fitzrovia Press
Glastonbury
www.fitzroviapress.co.uk

ISBN 978-0-9570722-1-3

printed and bound in Great Britain by Henry Ling Limited
at The Dorset Press, Dorchester
typeset in Centaur 12.5 point on 15.2
printed on FSC Olin High White Rough 80gsm

to my mother
Barbara Pamela
1924-2012
who passed into the arms of angels
as I began to write this book

other titles by Ranchor Prime:

Hinduism and Ecology
Ramayana: A Journey
Vedic Ecology
A Tale of Gods and Demons
Prince of Dharma: the Buddha
Mahavira: Prince of Peace
Hinduism
The Illustrated Bhagavad Gita
Cows and the Earth
Bhagavad Gita: Talks Between the Soul and God
When the Sun Shines: The Dawn of Hare Krishna in Britain
Birth of Kirtan: The Life and Teachings of Chaitanya

CONTENTS

Thank you...

Jörgen Sundval for helping me find the original inspiration; Ian and Andrea Roberts for giving me a place to write in the Lake District; Bhogini and Jon for their magical writing space and her help with the manuscript; my daughter Anna for her skilful editing; Lena for a peaceful home in which to work on this book; Peter Scarisbrick for his visionary friendship and patronage; Rhona Clews for guidance and healing; Nicole Hambro and Alchemy for a sacred space to explore the journey; Martin Palmer for his willing encouragement; my partner Anjana who arrived in time to help this book into the world; and, in Glastonbury where we found shelter together, Gareth Mills for his enthusiastic support; John Martineau for his helping hand; and Anthea Mitchell for her generous gift to print the book; and all the friends who read and commented on the manuscript along the way. On this journey of mystery, thank you all.

Earth, water, fire, air,
ether, mind, wisdom, ego—
these are my eight separated energies.

Krishna,
Bhagavad Gita
chapter 7 verse 4

THE CHOICE

The view from my window

CHANGE STARTS DEEP WITHIN. By the time it reaches the surface it has been with you longer than you know.

For years a quiet voice called me to change, though I wasn't ready to hear its call. It beckoned me into the fields and wooded hills surrounding London. I walked the country paths, under the trees or in the open with the wind and sun on my face, and felt in touch with a wholeness I didn't feel when I was in the city. As I walked I dreamed of another life. By my late fifties I had reached a plateau. I had lost my sense of direction and was meandering like a silted river. I thought I had probably done most of what I wanted and would drift through my remaining years. In my journal I wrote, 'I am at the end of a road that seems to lead nowhere.'

I didn't know that my life was about to change. An idea had been forming in my mind to publish books. Almost by accident I found myself launching my own publishing venture. I was excited by the challenge, but soon I was overwhelmed with stress and financial worries. As I turned sixty, one thing piled upon another. My marriage of thirty years came under strain. I witnessed one of my oldest and dearest friends die of a wasting disease, leaving me grieving not just for him, but for a life journey we had shared over four decades. I felt my faith ebbing away, and with it my energy. I had a growing sense of missing something in life, an unfulfilled potential, a spirit of adventure, and that I was now old. My meandering river plunged into rocks and rapids and I was gasping for air. I felt myself in crisis.

One day change broke to the surface. From nearly drowning in a turbulent current, I was thrown upon a sandy shore. The torrent rushed past me carrying with it the pieces of my life. I saw them disappear along with the worries that had filled my mind, leaving in their place a numbness and emptiness. I found myself in a place of silence and mystery.

When the way you are is no longer sustainable, when your life falls apart, change is not an option—it is a necessity. It may be frightening, confusing and unclear, but it is the only way left.

DEEPENING EXPERIENCE

In my lifetime I have watched our human family go through something like this process. Humanity has been in turbulence for many decades and the turbulence is getting worse. Despite the best efforts of visionary and dedicated people everywhere, we have entered a prolonged crisis with no end in sight. We are caught in a collective pursuit of material prosperity that will never be satisfied, that is creating for ourselves and our planet a catastrophe—a crisis of confidence, sustainability, well-being, social and political stability—a crisis of survival itself.

This is what we humans do. When at a deep level we have outgrown a way of being and we sense the need for change, we unconsciously push ourselves, just as I had in my personal life, further into that intense experience so as to bring ourselves to the moment of profound choice.

I believe we are pushing ourselves to deepen our experience of our human potential. Human life is not meant simply for experiencing physical nature made of earth, water, fire and air. We are also meant to inhabit the subtle realms of ether, mind, wisdom and ego. These elements underlie the visible world and our physical selves. Through these subtle elements we can come to know ourselves as eternal spirit, an experience which includes and transcends all the eight elements of nature.

This is the opportunity we are now choosing: to go beyond where we have been before and grow to a more complete understanding of who we are. In the past this experience was available to only a few rare individuals. Now our long journey through time and space has brought us to this place of choice, where we can step into the next plane of our collective universal experience.

I believe many of us hear this call—we hear it inside, calling us to fulfil our potential as humans and as spirits. The day this call returned to me, when my life changed for the second time, I felt utterly alone and abandoned.

EMPTINESS

I never experienced such emptiness before. As a child I don't remember feeling alone; whenever I was on my own I felt an invisible protective presence. Then, when I turned twenty, a friend introduced me to Krishna and I embraced the vision of God as a beautiful friend who danced and played the flute with other beautiful friends in an enchanted forest beyond time and space. From that day I held this image in my heart and started a new life.

Now, forty years on, Krishna left me. I felt myself alone in a vast empty wilderness. Overnight my world was void, my past evaporated; I no longer knew who I was or why I was alive. In this state I found it impossible to work. My life stalled—I was broken open, bewildered and lost. I tried to pray, but how do you pray when there doesn't seem to be anyone there? My wife and family, my friends, couldn't understand what I was experiencing. I could find no words to tell them because I didn't know myself. I knew only that I was broken and that I had enough tears inside me to fill an ocean.

My thoughts turned to my wise friend Jörgen Sundval, whose home overlooks Lake Vättern in Southern Sweden. He is a deeply gifted hypnotherapist and healer who had several times assured me of his full support if ever I needed help. I had never been ready to ask for help—I hadn't felt I needed it. Now I knew I did. I called him and without hesitation he invited me to come and stay. I boarded a plane and crossed the North Sea, feeling I was leaving my old life behind and flying into the unknown. Jörgen opened his home to me. Gently and lovingly, he took me on an inner journey that lasted two weeks. Every day we sat together while he guided me inward to understand myself and what was happening to me. With his help I poured out my emotions and was blessed to see many things and hear voices I will never forget.

SEEING THE CHOICE

One day I received a life-changing vision. I saw humanity at a crossroads and was shown the choice we are being given at this time on Earth. It was a vision of imminent disaster, but it also contained hope. The vision showed me a stark choice between light and dark, such as I have only encountered in visionary art and literature; I found it shocking, I have never seen life in such apocolyptic terms; but knowing the gravity of the world situation and the dangers we have created for ourselves, as well as the opportunities that beckon, I want to pass on what I saw and heard.

MY VISION

I felt myself bathed by healing energy in a field of endless blue space. I was supported by many unseen hands, embracing me with love.

I was shown the elements——carried downward into water which flowed over me, then immersed in earth and surrounded by fire.

I saw smoke and flames, darkness, with machines turning and spiralling in endless revolutions. I saw vegetation being burned up all around me, birds and creatures in distress seeking shelter in holes in the ground. All was wreathed in smoke and noxious fumes.

As far as I could see were smouldering flames, spread across the surface of a charred land. I saw no people. Where were the people? As soon as the thought arose the answer came, and I saw them beneath the ground, imprisoned inside the earth. They had lost their freedom by becoming slaves to machines. The people couldn't see the daylight. It was very sad to see.

I wondered if this devastation was everywhere, was there no hope? I was carried high into the air and shown in the distance a few patches of light. Coming closer I saw that amid this dead land were hidden valleys, places that were still green, where people were free. I saw communities living in light-filled settlements full of wisdom and love. They could see the sky, they had clear water and clean air. I saw that all was not lost. It was wonderful to see.

A voice spoke inside me giving a clear message.

There is a choice, the voice said. Everyone has this choice.

The choice lies between turning away from the light, feeding the machines, closing the doors, closing the windows to the vastness and the beauty and wonder of all of life. Ever-diminishing, this road leads to enslavement, destruction and pain—

Or choosing to seek the light, the daylight, pure water, clear air, growing things, the green; caring for the natural world, for the living beings, the creatures who are God's gift to us all to keep our minds open and clear. If we care for them, I was told, they will care for us. Then we can grow as we are meant to grow. In those valleys of light life flourishes. Life lived with the heart, life lived with spirit, wisdom and culture.

I was told to help guide people toward the light, toward the freshness and the clear air; help them see the beauty that they have in this world of nature.

I was told that we are approaching a time when the choice becomes more and more stark. The crisis will deepen. Voices of clarity must be heard, calling to those who can hear. There will be places where the spirit lives, but most places will become dark. This is happening already. In the places of light spiritual treasures can be found.

There is no need for humanity to build great castles or fill the world with machines, which only hurt the ones who are born here. They are the work of another force. They are a trap, I was told.

They represent the darkness, but they are here because the choice must be here. We are living in a time when everyone has the freedom to choose. That is the way the world is now, why the dark side is here, because people are being given choice at this time. In these times clear messages must be heard to enable the choice to be clear.

I was told to show the beauty and light that is in this perfect creation. To show that everything is here, all we need to live in peace, to live a simple life. Here we will find all truth, beauty, fulfilment, love.

Some are called upon to be voices of truth and clarity. It is a simple task, to hold the clear vision. Those who can will recognise it. They will hear and be encouraged, and they will find hope.

Again the choice was set before me.

The positive path is compassion, caring, humility, simplicity, cooperation, inspiration, kindness, growth and evolution, an unfolding story of increasing light and understanding; a wonderful opportunity is being given at this time.

The alternative is fear, narrowing, addiction, exploitation, cruelty, anger, withering of the spirit and, eventually, deep sleep. For those who cannot see the light will come the sleep of forgetfulness, when the light fades until another time, far, far away. It's like the seasons turning. So the world turns to withering and decay.

It is easy to find the people with vision, I was told. They are everywhere. Find them, encourage them, learn from them, help them, join them. Share this vision with them.

Show how the spirit lives in all life, calling to be loved and cared for. Learn that love and share it——through friendship, through music, words, visions, through being true and honest.

Then I was given a final message.

I was shown the wilderness in its natural state. After great damage had been done, I was told, after the darkness had been burned away, nature would return.

I saw that we are part of a larger story, that what we are experiencing now on earth is a passing phase. I saw that the process is never-ending. We go on a long journey and eventually we return to where we started. The journey is not a circle but a spiral. Each time the experience is new and we learn more.

FINDING INSPIRATION

In the days following this vision I was given the inspiration to write a book about the elements of nature, taking me on a journey through those elements to what lies beyond. As a place to start, I was pointed to a passage in the ancient source of wisdom, *Bhagavad Gita*. The passage lists the eight elements of nature as Krishna's energies. I protested that I knew very little about this subject, that I would hardly know where to begin. But I was told that the words would be given to me as I needed them, and that the meaning of the book would become clear as it progressed.

When I returned home to London my work began. My first task was just to survive each day, and to make sense of who I now was, since my old self had utterly gone. Amid my emptiness the conviction grew inside me that I had been blessed beyond measure—that I had been hollowed out, and the space inside me would gradually be filled with light, wisdom and joy. Having been stripped bare, I was to hold myself open and trust what I was to receive.

I entered a new kind of living in awareness of every moment, learning to feel myself, my body and my inner presence here and now; to feel and be with whomever was with me, to accept my life as a continuous adventure of discovery, each day a gift; to greet each experience, whether of comfort or pain, as a blessing; to greet all whom I met as my teachers and friends; to learn all over again how to live, how to be fully alive in every moment.

For a year my life stood still while I absorbed the changes in me and contemplated the book I was to write. Slowly ideas formed, visions and insights that I collected in scattered notes. I realised that until I wrote this book I would be unable to do anything else. I would have to put everything aside and give myself entirely to allowing the words to come through me. The moment I reached this decision my old friends Ian and Andrea offered me use of their cottage in the Lake District for six weeks. This, I hoped, would be long enough for me to get out a first draft.

INTO NATURE

So it was, in the late spring of 2012, that I came to Rydal to write about nature and the spirit. The view from my window stirred my soul. I could see over the tops of majestic redwood trees to distant Lake Windermere stretching south to the horizon. Framing the valley and lake were the fells, great mounds of rock and moorland, their wooded sides climbing to lofty crags.

The sky was a kaleidoscope of changing weather reflected on the surface of the lake. Some days the clouds collected along the valley floor, obscuring the hills and lake in a blanket of mist that merged with the sky. Other days the sun broke through to dapple hillsides with patterns of light and shadow, and sparkle on faraway waters.

Amid this magical landscape I meditated on nature and prayed for inspiration. As I wrote, I began to realise why I must write this book. Deep-rooted change is needed if human society is to survive the twenty-first century. More and more of us are realising that we cannot go on as we are, that we need to open ourselves to new understandings of human life on Earth; to find new inspiration for a way of living that encompasses the well-being of all nature—ourselves, our fellow humans, animals, all living creatures, the whole planet.

PROFOUND CHANGE

Before change can happen, a clear choice must be made. I believe we all have the freedom to choose the direction of our lives and the values we stand for. We have only to embrace our beliefs at a deep level and our path of change will open. Profound change begins in the heart. From the moment we embrace the clear intention for change, each of us according to our individual natures is inspired to act in a way to bring about a healthy and benign outcome. All life will conspire to bring this about. If enough of us decide to make the change, to surrender ourselves to it, transformation will happen. I have faith in our capacity, as beings of love, to transcend the challenges we face on Earth, should we choose to.

In this age, when relentless change and loss have brought our Earth family to a place of imminent danger, we have momentous choices to make. Here is my journey of discovery. This journey will make the choice clearer.

DISCOVERING THE ELEMENTS

Buckstones pool in Rydal Valley

Early one morning I set out from the cottage to walk up Rydal Valley. I wanted to immerse myself in the elements of nature so I could write about them. The valley was a wild place of wind, water and rock, inhabited only by mountain sheep. I climbed alongside Rydal Beck to a sheltered pool bordered on two sides by slabs of granite fissured with ancient seams and cracks. In its upper corner white water plunged down a steep diagonal channel worn smooth over thousands of years.

Scrambling down a grassy bank, I crossed stepping stones to an island of smooth pebbles in the centre of the pool. Above me cascaded water, filling the air with a continuous roar and sending waves radiating towards me. Patterns of ripples crisscrossed the sparkling waters, reflecting sunlight over glassy depths revealing a bed of multi-coloured rocks and stones. The flow gathered around me to race on between tall boulders and disappear down the valley. On either side mountain sheep cropped turf that climbed the valley sides amid a few hardy trees. Over the ridge a thousand feet above rose the sun, breaking in and out behind clouds drifting across a blue sky.

After a moment of hesitation in the chill morning air, I threw off my clothes and plunged into the icy water. My heart jumped and I could barely breathe. Forcing myself under I pushed into the foaming waves at the foot of the water chute, every nerve stinging as the cold started to bite. For two minutes I trod water and fought the current, gasping for breath. Then I turned back to the island and stumbled ashore, my body in shock and pain.

Naked and tingling I stood in the sun and wind as my circulation returned and my skin dried. I was exhilarated by immersion in raw and undiluted elements. Rocks glistened, sunlight warmed my skin, flecks of foam moistened my cheeks, aromas mingled in my nostrils, swirling sounds saturated my ears. I was held in nature's embrace, my five senses open and alive.

I dressed and settled cross-legged on the pebbles. Seated firmly, I closed my eyes and turned my gaze inward to feel the elements within.

At the base of my spine the foundation of solid earth supported me. I felt the rushing waters embrace the sacral area between my hips. Warmth from the sun spread across my stomach. The breeze tugged at my heart. The roar of the falls wrapped its vibration around my throat. Pulling my blanket tight in the crisp morning air, I held these elements inside and I remained there unmoving for twenty minutes, while the sun warmed my face and the wind ruffled my hair. Then I stood and headed back to the cottage for breakfast.

Making my way down the valley, now vividly aware of earth, water, fire, air and ether enveloping me on all sides, I contemplated the subtle elements of mind, wisdom and ego. My mind delighted in the panorama of natural beauty, triggering memories from a lifetime exploring hillsides and streams. My inner wisdom wondered at the majesty of nature and the mystery of life. In this pristine environment with its encompassing richness, my deep sense of self was awakened. I felt at one with the full spectrum of life focused in this place at this precise moment. An awareness rose from within.

I see, I taste, I smell, I touch, I breathe, I hear, I remember, I wonder—I feel one with the eight elements of nature, the ingredients of life on earth.

I am earth,
I am water,
I am fire,
I am air,
I am ether,

I am mind,

I am wisdom,

I am ego.

These coverings express my identity. They are the costume I wear and the stage upon which I move in the theatre of the mortal world.

The more I know these elements, experience them, understand them and meditate upon them, the more I know myself. They serve me by carrying my desires and expressing who I am, and who I wish to be. In turn I serve, honour and love them as energies of God. They are part of me and I am part of them.

And yet—I am beyond these. When I know them I can know nature's deepest secret. Beyond all this, before all this came to be and after it is dissolved…

I AM.

THE EIGHT ELEMENTS OF NATURE, as given in the ancient wisdom of the *Bhagavad Gita*, offer an alternative picture of reality, a way to conceive life in its full variety and depth. They have no precise equivalents in modern physics. Before I describe them let me first say that all nature is a manifestation of spirit. This world of mind and matter makes spirit visible. Therefore, I begin with the nature of spirit, namely love.

Love is the ultimate reality. It is what gives meaning to life, the essence of consciousness, the irresistible force that binds us together, that connects all life. Divine Love is the source of all there is. We are all part of this original source and we are made of love. This insight is sufficient to transform the world.

So how did the eight elements of nature come from love?

SPIRIT ENTERS MATTER

From the original source of love comes an infinite number of sparks, each the essence of a living being. Each being desires self-knowledge and so enters the world of ego. To know itself, ego generates wisdom. Wisdom gives rise to mind. Mind charged with emotion produces sound, which manifests ether and the sense of hearing. Ether becomes tangible and manifests air and the sense of touch. Air takes shape to manifest fire and the sense of vision. Fire engenders flavour, which manifests water and the sense of taste. Water generates odour, which manifests earth and the sense of smell. So arise eight elements with their corresponding senses, and so we, originally beings of pure love, come to experience ourselves as beings made of matter.

The physical elements of earth, water, fire, air and ether each possess distinct qualities. Air can be touched; fire can be touched and seen; water can be touched, seen and tasted; earth can be touched, seen, tasted and smelled. Mixed together, air, fire, water and earth make up the manifestation of nature that we can touch, taste, see and smell. To these is added ether, that can be heard. Ether links our inner and outer worlds. Our earthly bodies are thus made of five elements. These five are expressions of the finer elements of mind, that perceives the world; wisdom, that brings inspiration; and ego, that gives identity. Within all, animating all, is the spark of love that is the original self.

So we have the eight basic elements of nature, as taught in the ancient *Samkhya* philosophical system which is the basis of yoga. This way of understanding reality has been for me an invaluable guide to make sense of the experience of living on Earth.

LOSING FEAR

A question arises. How can a world originating from love include conflict? The reason is fear. When our mind creates a feeling of separation between us, showing other people as threatening to our ego, we experience fear, and from fear arises conflict. And when our mind tells us that we all share the same essence of spirit, that to love the other means to love myself and to love myself means to love the other, then we live in harmony. The whole journey of life is to bring us from fear to love—to the realisation that we can love every person we meet, whether friend or enemy, as much as we can love ourselves.

The more each of us realises this, the more we will find this world, every part of it, even the parts that cause us pain, to be manifestations of love. This love is the complete whole, the origin of the eight elements, and the mystery we are here to learn.

SHARING LOVE

My own journey of self-discovery began with love. When I was eighteen, studying at Chelsea School of Art, I fell in love with Julia. Her zest for life brought me adventure and helped me break free from the monastic influence of my boarding school days. Together we painted, visited art galleries, went to parties and enjoyed passionate love. But after two years, following a tearful argument, we broke off.

In the midst of this anguished scene I experienced an awakening; I saw myself bathed in spiritual light, lifted out of my ego and shown eternity. I felt as if the hand of God touched my brow. I said goodbye to Julia and withdrew into a contemplative lifestyle. Each morning I rose at six and walked three miles from my bedsit to the art school. My parents were divorcing and selling the family home, I felt alienated from the world, dissatisfied with what I saw as the shallowness of conventional things. I expressed my confusion and anguish by painting a succession of ever larger canvases.

For six months after losing the first love of my life I felt bleak and empty, as if a hollow opened inside me. Then I stumbled across the Krishna song. I picked it up from the soundtrack of the Hair musical that was playing in the West End. I was spending a last few weeks in our Sussex home, when my sister brought the record from London. I learned the words of the song not knowing what it was. They stole over me like the rays of the rising sun.

I walked all one summer's day over the heathlands of the Weald, losing myself in dense patches of gorse and fern. The mantra rose without my being aware of it. I found myself singing it in the valleys and hills. The sound strengthened me.

Like rain seeping into parched earth, like light flooding a darkened room, like the embrace of lovers——where does one end and the other begin?——so the emptiness I had been carrying came alive and embraced me from within. The mantra felt warm, substantial, a companion, a comfort and friend. I couldn't stop chanting——I didn't want to. For weeks it stayed with me until it became part of me.

I was reading Gurdjieff, Timothy Leary, Aldous Huxley, and was led to Krishna's poem of wisdom, the *Bhagavad Gita*. In Krishna's words I found solace, recognising in his voice the tender presence I had felt with me since childhood. Life has a way of arranging events. I now see I was guided through the emptiness of heartbreak to a course of spiritual learning, to the *Bhagavad Gita*, to the mantra and to Krishna. A close friend introduced me to the Hare Krishna people, who had just opened their mystical temple hidden in a small street in Bloomsbury. Arriving there felt like coming home.

I abandoned my art course, despite entreaties from friends, family and tutors. I was just starting my second year at Chelsea as a painter; art was my sacred calling; but I saw Krishna as the supreme artist who painted the sunrise, the birds and flowers, all the beauty of nature, the voice of wisdom. The vision of the Source of All as a child playing in nature, surrounded by creatures of the forest, in love with all life, filled my heart. I became a vegetarian, gave away my books and paintings, and moved in with the small community at the Radha Krishna Temple, where I began a new series of paintings.

I learned to meditate. I used to sit for hours chanting my mantra, visualising myself as spirit inside my physical body. I studied ancient yoga teachings and learned that my essen-

tial nature was eternal, conscious and joyful, *sat chit ananda.*
Through meditation I began to experience these qualities.

After a year in the ashram I met my guru, Bhaktivedanta
Swami, who came to stay with us in London. I had already
known him through his teachings, but when I spent time
with him in his room I felt a bond of personal affection
and my heart called me to serve him. He became everything
for me. By that time I was married to Serena, who had run
away from her prosperous home in South London to join
our community. My guru encouraged us to be spiritual
adventurers, so together we started a Krishna yoga centre in
Manchester.

Yoga meant for us the transformation of life through
love for the divine source of all. We felt our lives transformed and wanted to share that experience with others.
On our first day we went to the city centre, dressed in our
robes and saris, and sang sacred mantras. A crowd of
hundreds quickly gathered, smiling and laughing, filled
with curiosity. Within minutes a siren sounded, police
arrived, and we were herded into the back of a black van.
The people were disappointed and told the police to leave
us alone, but the young officers took us to the police
station where we were charged with disturbing the peace.

We wanted to share love and we met with opposition. I
didn't feel resentment, I just thought the police

misunderstood us. We were confronting them with something strange and unfamiliar, asking them to open up to a new experience, and their conditioning held them back.

In this world we all experience opposition in the form of birth, disease, old age and death. Illness, ageing and dying are not the nature of spirit, so they are difficult and painful experiences. It is only natural to have feelings of insecurity and fear, which can be triggered when we are confronted by the unfamiliar. It is a choice we all have, whether to open ourselves to new experiences or recoil from them. Love is opening up, fear is closing down.

In time the police came to learn from us. Groups of police cadets on community training sat patiently as we sang for them and told them about yoga. In those early days in Manchester I learned that no one is my enemy. The only disturbers of my peace are the negative thoughts inside my head. What I feel inside I project into the world. What I see outside is a reflection of what I feel inside.

DIVINE MOTHER AND FATHER

The religion I was brought up with worshipped God as a male creator who ruled the world and judged my actions. This has been the dominant God archetype of human religions for thousands of years. It gave sanction to a world dominated by men whose instincts were to rule and pass judgement, whose desire to control divided societies into conflict and exploitation. Our religions have been unable to take us beyond this pattern of control, despite the teachings of love they were founded upon, because they became repositories for fear and judgement. So they separated rather than united us, and they set humanity apart from nature.

I grew up believing in a Divine Father, who I thought of as my ever-present friend and still do, but I was less aware of my Divine Mother. I now know she was always with me, bringing me wholeness. My connection with the divine Mother is essential to my connection with life itself. She embraces me through the spirit of nature.

Forgetfulness of the Mother is reflected in our lost relationship with the Earth. Instead of receiving her embrace, we made her separate from us and tried to subdue her. This disconnection is the root of the imbalance that now threatens us all. Somewhere in our history we lost our intimate relationship with the Mother's embrace. Instead of seeing ourselves as her dependent children we believed we were her masters with the right to plunder her produce and victimise her children as if all of nature were our own to do with as we liked.

Now this has to change. We are on the cusp of that

change; but before the change can unfold we need to understand how deep the conditioning has been.

CHILDREN OF THE EARTH

Long ago our damaged relationship with the Mother led to three pathological tendencies embedded in human culture over thousands of years. They are: subjugation of women, enslavement of animals, and exploitation of nature. These three are symptoms of humanity's disconnection from the Mother. A mother cares for her children—but if they take from her by force, her nourishment is interrupted. This is what we see in the world today. Nature's abundance is everywhere, but we are creating scarcity.

We are nature's children, children of the Earth. Our urgent need is to heal our relationship with nature and so restore the balance of life. This healing happens at every level of our being, beginning from earth, through all the elements that we are made of to the subtlest life of our spirit. As wholeness manifests, our lives and the life of the world are transformed and illuminated in fullness and depth. This is the experience we are here to find in these challenging times, that will carry us to the unlimited gifts that lie ahead.

The journey through nature's eight elements deepens our connection with nature and with the love that is the basis of all life. It helps us discover ourselves. It may not make much sense yet: the elements are understood by experiencing them, and that is what this book is about. Knowledge of the eight elements shows how consciousness is present in all matter, and how this world is made of love. We don't just have to accept this as theory. The journey through the elements demonstrates their essence is love. It is like a pilgrimage: if we follow the road with heart it will change us.

The First Element

EARTH ❖ *Foundation*

My childhood home in the Sussex Weald

EARTH IS THE PLACE TO START. From where I will travel through the spectrum of elements, from dense to fine. Earth is the beginning of my journey because it is the core where my spirit is grounded in the cycle of birth and death. Our word for the element earth is also the name we give our planet. The same is true in Sanskrit: the name for both is Bhumi, and she is a living goddess. She is also Gaia, Terra and Pachamama: our mother and a manifestation of the universal Mother.

I grew up as a child of nature, roaming the countryside of the Sussex Weald. From my bedroom window I saw woodland and meadows receding in waves to the far crest of Crowborough Beacon, highest point in my world. When I was alone the outdoors was where I went for comfort, my cradle of nature, my Mother Earth.

I learned her folds and pathways, her hollows and streams. I felt safe among them, even after dark in the depths of the woods. Many times I walked through fading light beneath spreading branches of beech and oak, as owls hooted and shadows darkened. I picked my way through the undergrowth, stick in hand to push aside brambles, skipping from one patch of earth to another amid the forest bed of twigs, leaves and Wealden clay. I felt myself part of this place, the trees and creatures of the woods my friends, all born from the same rich earth.

The world of my youth was a gentle place, where nature enclosed me like the coarse woollen blankets of my bed. She had her dangers—oozing quagmires, sudden trenches, protruding roots, sharp rocks, rushing waters, and thorns that tore my flesh—but essentially she was kind, familiar and modest.

FRAGILE MAJESTY

When I was twelve years old I found a landscape on an altogether grander scale. With my school choir I was on my way to Loreto in Northern Italy, where we were to sing in a festival of sacred music and see with our own eyes the aged Pope John XXIII. As our sleeper train wound through the Swiss Alps the pale light of dawn revealed a magical world. While others slept I gazed at row upon row of mountain peaks climbing into the still air, their summits tipped with gold from the rising sun. They spoke to me of the heights of mystic wisdom, of worlds beyond my own.

To a child of the cosy Sussex countryside they beckoned with untold wonders.

At twenty I entered the spirit of those mountains when I discovered yoga, learned the philosophy of the Upanishads and stepped into a life of devotion to Krishna. I became vegetarian, hugged trees, saw nature as a conscious presence and sought to live in harmony with God's creation.

I began regular pilgrimages to India, and on one of those trips I encountered the Himalayas. Walking and cycling among their deep valleys I saw how the mountains exposed the crystalline skeleton of Mother Earth, their ridges crumbling, entire mountainsides slipping and breaking loose to plunge into fast moving waters on the valley floors.

I visited the town of Rishikesh, which sits at the gateway to the Himalayas on the banks of the Ganges. The riverbed was strewn with rocks worn smooth in her remorseless current, carried along until they were deposited on either side to form a spreading beach of boulders. The waters were thick with silt made of sparkling minerals. The mountains, so immovable and vast, were literally being washed away.

High above Rishikesh, in valleys hung with azalea, rhododendron, chestnut and pine, I wandered in the aromatic air. The ground beneath my feet bore the unmistakeable deposits of an ancient seabed. Compressed shells of tiny creatures glistened and crumbled where I trod. The sides of those massive mountains were composed of shifting layers of shale beneath a thin covering of forest humus.

I saw that although the Himalayas seemed solid and immovable, the mountains were alive in motion, their surfaces eroding as deeper layers shifted upward to show a new face. So mighty from afar, from nearby the Himalayas were fragile.

Planet Earth is the same. We take for granted that she is impervious to our actions, as if she will never change. But she is in perpetual change, and we are changing with her. What we do, how we treat and use her, affects us as it does her.

OUR ONLY HOME

Emotionally, I believe we are all in love with Mother Earth. She is everything we know. When the first astronauts went to the moon (or so we were told) I felt we were losing something, as if we were no longer held by Earth. Only a handful of men and rockets left Earth's gravity field, and only briefly, but they were backed by an army of scientists and engineers, by vast expenditure, by political propaganda and the longest running media story of the decade—all these gave the Apollo expeditions a global significance. At the time, in 1969, amid the poverty and chaos that affected most of our human family, the space race seemed to me a massive waste of resources. But the possibility of seeing the Earth from space and the radical new perspective it gave of our planet were transformative. The astronauts described what they saw.

'Standing on the moon, when I first looked back at Earth, I cried,' said Alan Shepard, commander of the Apollo 14 mission.

'As we got further and further away it diminished in size,' said James Irwin. 'Finally it shrank to the size of a marble, the most beautiful you can imagine. That warm, living object looked so fragile, so delicate, that if you touched it with a finger it would crumble and fall apart. Seeing this has to change a man.'

I can only imagine how they felt to be away from Earth, but I do know how I feel to witness all around me the slow disintegration of Earth's eco-systems as our species dismantles the delicate balance of Earth's biosphere. I ponder the irony—this slender biosphere wrapped around the surface of the globe is all that separates us from endless space; it is our home, the source of our life—yet we are busy destroying it.

AMONG THE TREES

My way of feeling Mother Earth is to walk among her trees. There I immerse myself in Earth's embrace. Growing in her rich soil, trees draw her living energy out into the open where it can be shared in abundance.

Entering the woods this autumn, I felt a hush descend. Sunlight dappled the drifting leaves crunching under my feet; above me, arched branches supported a green tent beneath a pale sky. I felt life all around; a hooting owl, the call of a woodcock, the distant coo of a wood pigeon; the community of birds, forest creatures and trees gathered to hold me. Earth's energy rose through my feet and claimed me. Mother, I thought, I belong to you, one amongst your vast family, a drop in your vibrating ocean of life.

My relationship with trees has changed. When I was a boy they were playgrounds to climb and scratch initials on. Then I discovered they had a life of their own, though I knew little of it. For a decade I worked to preserve trees and woodland in India——trees were to be protected and appreciated for their environmental value. Now I see them as wise companions who teach me, especially the old trees of London, who have lived here for hundreds of years and are more part of this place than I: the fifty-foot plane trees that adorn the parks, the hoary oaks of Hampstead Heath and the ancient yews, dating back two millennia or more, that sleep on the fringes of the city. One hollow beech in the woods near Highgate has room for five adults in its womblike interior, polished smooth as a church bench by centuries of residents. It is my place of pilgrimage.

Trees spend their time rooted in deep slumber, changing only slowly in response to the seasons. Patiently they spread their branches into the air, draw in carbon dioxide and sunlight, blossom and bloom, fruit and seed, give shelter to countless creatures, silently grow and move, connect with one another, root ever deeper into the earth, reach upward and outward further into the space around them. While doing all this their movement is imperceptible. Almost motionless, they are silent reminders of inner stillness, of Krishna's words, 'The wise see non-action in action, and action in non-action.'

Standing in one place, feeding on soil, rain, sun and air, they drop their leaves, which turn to mulch and feed the earth. In course of time the trees also drop, their huge forms crashing to earth, where their decaying mass gives rise to new life.

Trees give me that place of stillness where I can be in touch with the spirit of Mother Earth and gain strength from her. From this position of strength I can grow to be patient, tolerant and giving, as trees are. I can do this when I am rooted in harmony with nature.

EARTH'S PULL

As I walk upon the surface of Earth I am mostly unaware of how I draw energy from deep within her. A magnetic force coming from her core rises to her surface and spreads out into space. We her children are radiated with that life-giving energy.

We feel our attraction to Earth at its most basic level as gravity. Modern science cannot explain gravity. We only know that Earth, with all heavenly bodies, emits a force that attracts other bodies. I think of this attraction as a manifestation of her love and our dependence on her. As well as attracting our physical bodies, Earth attracts our minds and subtle beings. We are tied to her as children to their mother. Our thoughts naturally return to her, our lives are circumscribed by her.

If you focus your attention, you can feel your connection to Earth as a flow of energy, a subtle transmission that passes from Earth to all her children. A tingling energetic presence enters through your feet. If you stay still for a moment, you can feel this connecting energy passing into your energetic body. Because this vibration has been with you since birth you have become accustomed to it, and most of the time it goes unnoticed.

Once you discover this energetic bond you can consciously draw strength from it. I feel it flowing up my legs to the base of my spine, where my first chakra is situated. Chakra is the Sanskrit name given to the vortices around which subtle energy flows through the body. The word means 'wheel' because energy moves round each chakra in a circular way, spiralling between the seven chakras. The first chakra, called the root, is the seat of physical energy. From here the flow continues up, swirling around the spinal column, bringing life, strength and balance. So Mother Earth fills us with her energy and her love.

HEALING CRYSTALS

For those who are sensitive to it, a subtle manifestation of Earth's force field can be experienced in working with healing stones.

On the hillside paths in the Lake District I find the ground carpeted with broken stones. At first sight they appear a monotonous grey, but when I look closer I see each one has its own unique colour, texture, pattern and shape. No two are the same. When they are washed into the streams, tumbled and rolled along for a few thousand years, they transform into smooth pebbles. Their subtle colourings glisten under the clear water of mountain streams. Through such fragments of herself Mother Earth transmits her concentrated essence in the form of healing crystals and stones.

The earth delivers these stones to us in riverbeds, eroded from rocky outcrops, beneath tree roots or just lying on the ground. When they are handled with sensitivity their presence assists in healing the body, focusing the mind, soothing the heart and stimulating the intellect.

In the last few years I have become more sensitive to the energetic properties of stones and crystals. Accounts of the properties of particular stones vary from one individual to another. Rather than repeat someone else's impressions I preferred to discover for myself, so I assembled a small collection of stones and sat quietly holding each one to feel its presence.

I began with Malachite, which has a luminous bluish green colour. In the morning before meditating I held the small stone in the palm of my hand and closed my eyes, allowing my mind to tune into the energy of the stone. I felt calmed and strengthened, as if I were being grounded and balanced. My focus became clearer, more determined, and I felt whole. It seemed to me that Malachite could help reduce stress, and perhaps lower my high blood pressure, and that it might improve my digestion. I was surprised to feel all this by holding a stone. But then I reflected that Earth is a goddess and it would be quite natural to feel aspects of her conscious presence in these stones.

The next day I tried Selenite, a whitish stone with a distinctive parallel grain revealing translucent depths. It gave me a feeling of clarity and focus, enhancing my inner vision. I felt my memory and brain sharpened. A feeling of peace stole over me. I felt that it would be a great help in reducing stress.

I held a small piece of Lapis Lazuli, with its deep blue colour, and felt a sense of alertness and clarity, with a penetrating awareness to see into other's minds.

Moonstone is the colour of a soft shining moon, with smoky depths. It gave me a soothing sense of calm and acceptance. It would help me when I have a headache.

I tried others – Turquoise aided my communication, Amethyst opened my third eye and my intuition, Tiger's Eye filled me with warmth and friendship.

Friends told that Rose Quartz has a warm, loving presence. I found the same and always have it with me.

Other stones I have are Jade, Hematite, Citrine, Amber and Clear Crystal. Rather than tell you what affect they have I invite you to experiment for yourself, with an open mind and heart, and see what you find.

EARTH GODDESS

Earth gives us everything, and like children we often take from her without giving in return. We need to practice gratitude. Here is an ancient Sanskrit mantra of gratitude traditionally sung to her at the start of day.

prithvi tvaya dhrita loka
devi tvam vishnuna dhrita
tvam ca dharaya mam nityam
pavitram casanam kuru

Mother Earth, you support all beings
Goddess, you are maintained by Vishnu
Please always maintain me
And bless this place

This prayer mentions Vishnu as the creator father who sustains Mother Earth, whose name is given as Prithvi. She cares for her children, making no distinction between one species or another. All her creatures, great or small, call forth her love and abundant gifts. If we are confident that our mother is supplying our needs, then no matter how little we have we will live peacefully. We will feel ourselves part of her vast family and be secure. With this instinctive sense of trust our lives will be peaceful. On the other hand, if we harm Earth or her children, and take more than we need without gratitude and without giving back, we will not feel this sense of security. No matter how much we own or control we will not find peace.

A primary way to practice awareness of Earth's love and generosity is to thank her for the abundance of food she gives us. The ancients knew this and made food the focus of prayer and worship. Since eating and drinking are the foundation for sustaining life on Earth, the way we produce our food, prepare and eat it is crucial to our quality of life. Modern industrial food production depends on mechanical irrigation, heavy machinery, use of fossil fuels, monoculture and cruelty to animals. When food is brought to us through a cycle of violence it carries the influence of that violence into every aspect of our lives and societies. Food produced this way poisons our way of life at the very root.

On the other hand, food that is locally produced with care, without violence to the Earth or her creatures, that is prepared and served with a spirit of gratitude and love, becomes food not only for the body but also to uplift the spirit. The ancient custom of grace before meals, of actually speaking words of thanks over food, is a powerful spiritual practice to restore food's essential healing qualities and a regular reminder during the daily rhythm of life to bring our awareness back to the source.

PLEASE AND THANK YOU

The organic food movement draws attention to the deep need to find gentler ways to produce our food. People in locally connected networks are starting a revolution in the food cycle. This can involve rediscovering the ancient festivals like Wassail, which says 'please' at the start of the year; and Lammas, which says 'thank you' at the time of harvest. Festivals like these were part of cultures all over the world, but have been swept away by modern farming practices. If we are to find peace and harmony, a profound change will have to come about in the global production of food.

One day on returning home from shopping, I unpacked my provisions and spread them out on my kitchen table. I sat down for a moment to acknowledge the presence of the food, to feel its collective energy as the gift of Mother Earth. Reflecting on each item, I visualised where it came from, the nourishment it received from sun, rain and earth, the work of those who grew and harvested it, the hands that packaged it and brought it to market. If some of the food was of questionable provenance or less than ethically produced, I noticed that and accepted it to be so. Perhaps in future I would reconsider that purchase; nevertheless I accepted it with gratitude.

I give thanks for the blessings of Mother Earth while preparing meals, and before I eat I pause to express my gratitude and so bless my food. A Scottish minister taught me the world's simplest grace, 'Ta pa'——thank you father. Or you might say, 'Ta ma.'

EARTH SANCTUARIES

When I walk in the countryside to reconnect with the earth, I try to include a visit to an ancient church. England is blessed with many thousands of these hallowed buildings, one in nearly every village, and their doors are usually open to anyone who cares to enter. Inside I sit silently and feel the centuries of prayer and belonging to the land. Beneath their floors and all around are bones of the ancestors, candles burning, sunlight shining through stained glass enriched with sacred images. These places feel to me like home. They restore my spirit.

Humans have always honoured sacred places. Some, such as the Celtic Druids in their groves or the forest sages of India, gathered among trees because to be among trees was to be enclosed and roofed over. Others hollowed out the earth to make stone-sided tombs and burial mounds. Elsewhere humans made stone circles or piled stones into pyramids, drawing earth's energy into the sky and calling down cosmic energy from the heavens.

Early churches in England were built of wood, later to be renewed in stone. This meant our early architectural forms had their origin in nature's forms in the forest. The nave of a gothic church with arched pillars meeting in the roof imitates the trunks of trees rising to arched branches above the forest floor. When I stand in a great cathedral beneath its pillars and arches I feel as if Earth is emerging from the stone floor through stone columns to spread her canopy of stone or wood high above me. Some of these canopies have stood for more than a thousand years. They manifest a power and presence that embraces and nourishes the spirit of prayer they enclose.

My love of churches is rooted in my childhood. I lived four years as a choirboy in the precincts of Westminster Cathedral, built at the end of the Victorian Age on a vast scale to be the mother church of Roman Catholic England. We sang the daily Latin office from our choir stalls behind the high altar. Our days began before dawn with mass in the crypt. There, in a vault encircled with relics in gilded cabinets, we kept company with generations of entombed cardinals whose faded crimson hats hung from the ceiling.

The processions, the cycle of feast days, the daily round of prayer and liturgy, the encompassing history that stretched from Biblical origins to the yet undimmed magnificence of the Church of Rome peopled with nuns, priests, monsignors and archbishops—the dead cardinals supplying the final mark of authenticity—all these filled my unformed mind with a sense of divine purpose.

HUMAN-MADE FORMS

These great temples and cathedrals built in brick and stone, that evolved from simpler forms of wood and earth, mirror the evolution of the human spirit in our cycle of human history. Humans saw Earth as sacred, and formed her into icons expressing their wish to be connected to the spirit of the universe. They made divine images in stone, at first carved in relief on cave walls, later in freestanding stone figures around which temples arose.

Human structures in timber and stone expressed our consciousness. At first we built with mud, brick or stone; we added iron and copper to our buildings; then steel and concrete. Where once our buildings were hand-formed with irregular human-shaped surfaces, now they have become flat, rectangular, hard-edged and lifeless, reflecting the machinery and materials used to manufacture them. Our settlements, once gathered around temples and churches, are now dominated by factories, office blocks and shopping malls, tangled in road networks that obliterate the living surface of the earth.

Over time the human scale of our buildings has been lost. Our architecture that once belonged to the land now imposes upon it; buildings that once reflected nature's forms now express alienation from our natural surroundings. We need to rediscover our heart connection with the Earth.

FEELING EARTH'S ENERGIES

At home I have a meditation room. There I keep a small piece of stone about the size and shape of my heart. It is a fragment of Govardhan, a hill in India sacred to Krishna. With other pilgrims I have walked barefoot around this hill, setting off early in the morning to avoid the midday heat. The rising sun illuminates the marbled eastern escarpment with a peach-coloured glow. One day as I watched the shifting early morning light I felt waves of energy radiating from the hill. I saw them ripple above the crest and descend to bathe me and the other pilgrims, washing us in the hill's sacred aura. That was when I understood why so many people journey from far away to be near it.

I found a profound beauty in Govardhan. The hill is not large, but it has an imposing presence as it rises from the level plain. The surrounding landscape, scattered with sacred ponds and groves, each with its local shrine between fields of wheat and sugarcane fed by waters from the Yamuna, is a living temple to Krishna and his goddess Radha. Here nature shows herself as home of the divine.

Such energies are all around us, radiating from the Earth, as gravity, as magnetic attraction and as healing patterns of love. Once in a while, in a special place like Govardhan, or in some other display of Earth's abundant beauty, I recognise her wondrous embrace.

HIMALAYAN FOREST

Another such moment came upon me when I was in the Himalayan forest. My path wound round vertical cliffs that soared above me on both sides with the Ganges far below. I felt I was penetrating a realm beyond time. I reached an ancient village cradled in a pine-clad valley hanging two thousand feet above the river. The houses were made of stone and wood, and looked as if they had hardly changed in a thousand years. A shepherd boy pointed me to a footpath which climbed toward distant ridges.

I walked and scrambled up through rocks and tree-roots, hearing behind me the faint sound of the river echoing through the mountains. The Ganges is revered by Hindus as a goddess. In the mountains it is easy to see why, as she courses far below. I saw only an occasional glimpse of her glistening stream, appearing as a thread of turquoise hidden in the valley floor. I reflected how strange it was that a place so far from my homeland should feel so much like home.

I climbed until I reached a smooth slab of rock giving me a broad view of the valley and distant snow-capped peaks. In the warm spring sunshine I sat intoxicated by forest scents of pine and tree blossoms, the air rich with buzzing insects and butterflies of every hue. Beneath the high-pitched call of birds and the moan of the wind through the pines, the voice of the Ganges called to me.

Under my feet was the fragile debris of the mountains. I gathered a handful which I still have in a sealed glass jar by my shrine. The mystic life, which thrives in such remote places, is grounded in the earth on which we walk. Whether it be the aromatic ingredients of a Himalayan forest floor or the damp leaf mould of the Sussex Weald, that earth is the support from which we grow, the base upon which we depend, the stage for the drama of our lives.

In the magical heights of the Himalayas, held in the awesome splendour of Mother Earth's wonders, I felt earth was my rock and firm foundation; and I felt the river's flowing movement express my restless energy. I was moved from earth to water, the next of the eight elements.

EARTH MEDITATION

Sit with both feet flat upon the ground, or sit cross legged on the floor, or on a cushion on the floor.

Any surface that supports you is 'earthed' and conducts Earth's energy to you.

Concentrate on the sensation of the ground beneath your feet or beneath the base of your spine.

Feel the vibration of Earth's energy.

Focus on the flow of this energy as it rises through your legs, or directly into your base and up your spine.

Feel this energy as the love of Mother Earth always embracing you.

Allow yourself to feel gratitude for her constant support.

TREE MEDITATION

Find a tree, or visualise being with a favourite tree. Stand beneath it with your feet planted firmly apart.

Extend one hand to touch the trunk and feel the texture of its bark. Place your other hand over your heart.

Visualise the tree's roots radiating from the base, their fine silvery fibres penetrating deep into the ground. Feel Earth's energy rising through them into the trunk and branches.

Notice the ground on which you and the tree stand. You are both drawing energy from this ground. You both have unseen channels linking you deep into the earth. Feel the energy rising like sap through your legs and toward your heart.

Now visualise the tree's branches reaching upward to draw energy from the sun. Feel this energy from the sun pouring into you and reaching your heart. The descending energy combines in your heart with the energy rising from Earth.

All earthly life exists in this meeting place between Earth and Sky. You, the tree, all living beings, receive from Earth and from Sky. Notice their power. Feel their protective embrace merge within you.

The Second Element

WATER ❖ *Flow*

Rydal Falls

I HAVE CLIMBED THROUGH THE WOODS to Rydal Falls, hidden in the steep-sided gorge above the cottage. The mossy ledge where I stand is only a dozen feet from the torrent. White water churns past me down a twenty foot drop, bouncing off jagged rocks and sending vibrations rippling through the air. I feel something like an electric charge from the water, filling me with vigour and alertness.

In the valley above these woods rainwater merges into boggy upland turf. The peat and thick-rooted tufts of grass hold it like a sponge, releasing it to seep down the hillside in rivulets that join with others, until they meet in Rydal Beck and tumble through rocky outcrops, pour over boulders, gathering more and more water to become this thundering torrent, which cuts into the ancient rocks that tower either side of me as it plunges into a dark and forbidding pool, scooped out at the foot of the falls beneath me.

On the valley floor further down, other streams bring their own rushing waters to merge into a broad river, strewn with boulders, which winds through pastures and woodland until it spills into the majesty of Lake Windermere, stretching twelve miles into the hazy distance, giving life to the whole teeming landscape.

I love to be beside a river, especially a wild mountain stream. I could watch the flowing water for hours. An untamed river connects me to the ever-present flow of the spirit. As the river flows through the panorama of life, so the stream of spirit flows through me. As the valley with its trees and wildlife comes alive in the presence of a river, so my life is nourished by the spirit that courses within me and unites us all. If I look beneath the surface of life I find that mysterious river, I hear it echo through the world and through my life. Always alive, always flowing, the spirit is never still.

ENDLESS MOTION

All life forms are fluid, mostly made of water. The rock and soil of Earth's surface are firm, whereas the waters are always moving. Since water's nature is to be fluid, it imparts this quality to life forms. Living creatures are always in motion. From earth comes our stability, from water our movement.

We have this fluid nature inside us, particularly in that part of our bodies that holds our organs of creation and release, the seat of our sexuality. This is where we feel our connection with the water element.

The energy held in this sacral area can be a burden to carry. In my youth I was taught to fear sexual desire as something shameful. In later years I was blessed with the joyful feelings that come from being a channel of this creative energy that flows in all life. I also tasted that side of sexuality that leads to emptiness. I no longer fear sex, though I am in awe of its mysterious force. Like flowing water it is inviting and sometimes perilous. It is deep magic.

We begin life in this sacral area, immersed in the fluid of our mother's womb, hence we are forever comforted in water. Immersion in a stream refreshes tired limbs and clears the mind; floating in warm water brings relaxation—a return to source. To swim in rivers, lakes or the ocean brings vigour, clarity and health.

My childhood fascination with water led me to the woodland streams. I waded the shallows to collect stones and fallen branches for building dams and making water-falls and rapids. Standing midstream, I exulted in the energy of the river flowing around me and leaking into my boots.

My mother wanted me to overcome my fear of deep water and learn to swim. For my ninth birthday, on holiday in Spain, she gave me goggles and flippers. I spent hours in the sun-soaked shallows of the Mediterranean exploring the seabed, face down, propelled by my flippers, absorbed in miniature aquatic life——shrimps, crabs, shellfish, tiddlers and seaweed. Lapped by gentle surf, I drifted deeper into the waves. The ocean called me to her warm embrace. Before I knew it I could swim. In time water taught me that most magical of skills——to let go, surrender to the current of life and allow it to carry me wherever it wished.

PLANET OF WATER

Earth is wrapped in the ever moving embrace of water. The oceans covering two-thirds of her surface are her stock of water, kept salty to maintain their purity——salt is a disinfectant. Before seawater can be drunk it must be desalinated. The sun does this, evaporating salt water from the oceans and carrying it over the land as clouds to deposit distilled water on hills and mountains. The uplands absorb rain and store it in their underground reservoirs, capturing some of it as ice and snow to be released as melting water through the summer months. Surface water and springs feed the rivers, which bring life to the land before finding their way back to the sea. So the water cycle is complete.

In water's circulation is the ceaseless flow of life——our revolving days and nights, the passage of seasons, our accumulating years——carrying us ever onward. No experience is ever repeated. We grow through childhood, fall in love, watch our own children grow, experience the broad valley of life and die. Death is not the end; it is another beginning. If we wish, we may return to earthly life, or journey to other realms and experience ourselves and God's blessings in other ways. The adventure never ends.

Water has its moods and colours. It can be clear and still, full of peace and comfort, or it can be a life-threatening force. Water shapes mountains, valleys and plains; when it is in flood nothing can withstand its power. The majesty of the ocean swell echoes the life-giving rhythms of the planet, while a tsunami shows an awesome face of nature that flattens everything in its path. Water vapour can drive a tropical storm bringing floods and destruction, yet it also clothes the land in mists and fog, or drenches hillsides with rain-soaked clouds.

I remember the exhilaration I felt as a child running out into the rain and being soaked to the skin. Indoors, warm and dry, I still thrill to the patter of raindrops on a roof, or the drumming of heavy rain that reveals the shape of the landscape. Amid the dense wash of sound I see not with my eyes but with my ears, as rain drenches trees and bushes, strikes a tin roof, lashes against a wall, rushes down gutters, drips from overhangs, gurgles into channels and disappears into drains and ditches, weaving a tapestry of sound that immerses me in nature's ocean.

LIFE IN THE FLOW

I was swept into the flow of the spirit when, after two years studying architecture, I switched to Chelsea School of Art to study painting. I was disenchanted with materialism, and entered a spiritual search for meaning. Like many of my contemporaries, I experimented with LSD. My fourth psychedelic experience was going to be my last. I hitchhiked north to Scotland, wanting to meet God in a remote and exposed place—I pictured myself alone on a rocky cliff above a tempestuous sea—but it was in the forest above Inverness that I broke through my fears to enter a place of inner peace and connection with nature and God. I walked down off the hilltops into the town, and ended the day in an empty church feeling a profound sense of God's presence. I thought I would have no more need for LSD—it had shown me what I needed to learn. However, there remained one more lesson.

A month later, on my twentieth birthday, three of my friends took me to the borders of Kent and Sussex where I grew up. As darkness fell it began to rain. We entered the forest and settled among dripping pines in one of the caves in the sandstone ridge of the Weald. We lit candles and took the best quality LSD my friends could buy. I had been reading Timothy Leary's manual *The Psychedelic Experience*, in which he gave advice to assist explorers as they journeyed into the unknown. While my friends became talkative and excited, I followed Leary's advice to sit in silence, my attention withdrawn from all external distractions and focused on my breathing. In my mind my prayer was the same as before, to meet God. I saw the surface of life dissolve into infinite patterns of light and colour, pulsating with the primeval energy of creation. I felt myself one with everything. My ego dissolved. I wandered into the forest alone and unafraid. Although it was a dark night I saw everything clearly by an ethereal light. I followed a sandy path into the depths of the woods, and there amid a golden light I met an overwhelming divine presence of tender love.

That night of visions transformed my life and propelled me toward the spirit. Two weeks later I moved in with the Krishna people. I had no idea where I would be led. I followed my inspiration, leaving behind all thoughts of career or money. My days were made of serving, meditating, singing, and telling people about Krishna. After a year in the London ashram I moved to Manchester where I spent my days either on the street singing and selling magazines, or visiting schools, colleges, private homes, yoga societies—wherever would have me, to talk and sing about

Krishna. That period of my life lasted seven years during which I hardly paused for breath. It took me to India, to California, to Kenya and back to London. I was like a river with an endless flow of energy passing through me.

STAYING CLOSE TO WATER

In the modern age we have lost touch with flowing water, and the disconnection has impoverished us. People in every community, sometimes every household, were once involved in collecting their own water and safeguarding their water sources. Local springs, wells and streams were given almost sacred status. With the growth of urban living we were separated from our rivers and wells, and the spiritual traditions associated with water were forgotten. In a few places the old memories still linger. Sacred wells are again becoming centres for healing, meeting and blessing as they were in ancient times. In their ceremonies, some still invoke the purifying power of water and its capacity to connect us to the spirit.

Here in England the days when people drew their water directly from rivers or lakes are long gone. Yet the further our lifestyle is removed from natural water sources, and the more dependent we are on the invisible network of piped water and well-engineered drains and sanitation, the more we long for what we have lost. Instinctively we feel the absence of living water. The day must surely come when our communities are once more connected to their local water sources, only this time with a more complete under-standing of water's power to purify our lives and our consciousness.

While I am staying in the Lake District the water in my tap comes straight off the hillside behind the house. It tastes of the minerals of the hills, and carries the spirit of this place. As I drink it and the water runs through my body, I am tied closer to the landscape around me. I am also made aware that I don't want to waste this water. Being dependent on a natural spring teaches me to be responsible for using the water well. During a dry spell the watertable here drops and residents have to ration themselves. While I am here I share in this direct relationship with the water and the consequences of the local weather. This means so much more than simply turning on a tap and having no relationship with my water supply.

It is easy to see the healing effect of water on the mind by observing how people are drawn to seek peace and harmony beside water. Habitations grow up by rivers and lakes or by the sea; the most sought-after homes overlook water. In cities across the developed world, as dockyards fall into disuse, former dockside and canal-side sites are in demand as places to live. Seashores, lakesides, river banks—these are places where we go for inspiration, to rest and seek rejuvenation.

WATER AND CONSCIOUSNESS

When water flows as it does in nature—swirling, spiralling, bubbling and meandering across the earth's surface, absorbing minerals, sunlight and air—its flow is the dance of life. But when we force it into pipes and pump it at high pressure through water supply grids, enslave it to industrial plants and fill it with toxins, keeping it trapped behind valves and taps ready on demand to serve our needs—when we do this we imprison water and neutralise its healing energy.

Inspired researchers in the twentieth century explored these qualities in water. Viktor Schauberger, who started life as a forester in Austria, devoted himself to exploring the energies carried in water, and how water can be kept alive and enhanced through flow. Jacques Benveniste risked his reputation as a senior member of France's Academy of Sciences to publish his pioneering experiments proving that water carries memory. Masaru Emoto in Japan further showed water's conscious qualities by exposing it to positive intentions such as gratitude, or negative intentions such as anger, then photographing its molecular structure in ice crystals. His photographs showed that the shape of the crystals expressed the harmony of positive emotions or the disharmony of negative emotions.

As a Catholic schoolboy I was taught to sanctify myself with water. Before entering a church I dipped my fingers in the bowl of holy water by the entrance, then made the sign of the cross—forehead, heart, left shoulder, right shoulder—with the words 'in the name of the Father, the Son and the Holy Ghost, amen.' This ritual gave me a sacred connection with water. Years later I heard Krishna's words in the *Bhagavad Gita*, 'I am the taste of water.' I had not thought of water as having a taste, but then I realised its taste was spread everywhere, in everything, the basis of all taste, and because of this its taste had disappeared.

I learned to bless water with the name of Vishnu: '*Sri Vishnu, Sri Vishnu, Sri Vishnu*,' letting the name resonate in a moment of stillness as I held a cup to my lips before tasting. Along with the water something else entered, an invisible divine presence that is also spread everywhere, like the taste of water.

One day in a friend's kitchen I saw the words 'love' and 'gratitude' written on a piece of paper stuck to the side of her water jug. She told me how she believed water carried memory and responded to positive emotions—it remembered love. This made perfect sense to me and gave fresh meaning to my practice of reciting the Vishnu mantra before drinking. I wrote those words on my own water jug and deepened my commitment to blessing food and water.

Human bodies are said to be between 50 and 75 percent water. This means the conscious quality of water we drink affects our inner state. Similarly our food has a high water content. The way we treat water is at the root of how we produce food. The consciousness with which food is prepared affects its vibrational quality. Food and drink prepared with gratitude and love have a powerful cleansing effect on the body and mind.

Mystics have long known that water carries consciousness. To bless water is as old as religious faith. Sacred wells and springs, sacred rivers and bathing places, are part of human culture. Water carries the consciousness that surrounds it. When water is blessed, it imparts healing. The ancient Hindu practice of blessing water with the name of Vishnu is paralleled in Europe where for a thousand years water has been blessed with the Latin words, *ut quidquid hæc unda resperserit, careat omni liberetur immunditia a noxa*, 'whatever this water touches, let it be freed from all that is harmful or unclean.'

Water reflects our intentions back to us. Whether we use a name of God, a prayer, or thoughts of love and gratitude, we are acknowledging the gift of water. Water addressed with such attention and awareness heals us in body, mind and spirit.

MIXING WITH THE WORLD

In 1973 I was living with my wife in a squat in Notting Hill, London. We had occupied the basement of a large old house, painted it with bright colours and invited people to chant with us and share our meals. Every Saturday we ran a stall in nearby Portobello Market, where we sold Indian beads, incense and clothing, and distributed vegetarian food in exchange for donations. This gave us sufficient—we needed hardly any money.

George Harrison had just given the Krishna community a large manor house in the countryside north of London. That summer my guru stayed there for two months, and whenever I could I made the journey to hear him speak. On one occasion, as usual, I took an early train to the local station in Hertfordshire and walked a mile and a half over the heath. I arrived to find the main room filled with singing and dancing devotees. The atmosphere was charged with ecstasy. Everyone danced in their own spontaneous way, united in a wave of energy that filled the room. As I joined them I felt us floating in an ocean of sublime joy, our feet barely touching the ground. I am so thankful to my guru for introducing me to this practice of kirtan. He gave me one of my life's great gifts, to dance and sing in conscious awareness of myself as an eternal spirit. In giving myself to the dance and to the sacred chanting, I was lifted to a level of consciousness far beyond my LSD experiences. Regular practice of kirtan was how I learned to stay in the flow, the dance of life.

When I look back on those years I wonder at the young man I was, so ardent in his dedication, so undeterred in his conviction, broadcasting the message of Krishna. I am amazed at the dedication I had, but I also see a certain intolerance in my youthful self; an inability to accommodate views contrary to my own. I so utterly became the message that in the process I lost touch with parts of myself, the parts I couldn't allow into the open because they might take me away from my spiritual path. Sometimes they manifested in disturbed dreams, or outbursts of anger. As much as I loved the image of my holy teacher who I was trying to emulate, I came to fear those suppressed parts of myself.

I thought if I just tried harder—kept renewing my determination, making lists of goals, working out schedules to use my time better, getting up ever earlier in the morning to throw myself with more intensity into my chanting and study—I would be able to root out those hateful bits of me. Sometimes it almost seemed that I was winning; for a few days, weeks, maybe even months. Then all of a sudden my fragmented ego would come crashing back bringing with it a bitter resignation: perhaps I would never change.

I now know that change takes its own time. It cannot be forced. Those difficult parts of myself are like stones in the riverbed. They also need to be loved. In time the steady flow of water will wear them smooth and soften their sharp edges. Once in a while an inundation may sweep away even great obstacles to transform my inner landscape. In the meantime I need to be patient, changing what I can and accepting what I cannot, and trusting for the rest in the infinite love of God.

Serving My Guru

Before starting art college I had trained briefly as an architect. Learning of this my guru began giving me directions about how he would like temples to be built. At the time I couldn't do much beyond making drawings and models. It was not until he lay dying in India that the opportunity came to begin work on a new temple in London. We had bought a dilapidated building in Soho. I poured my grief at losing him into converting the place to a house of prayer, a home for Radha and Krishna, and an ashram for their devotees. My upbringing among churches and monasteries found expression in designing and building a temple and ashram for Krishna, with a vegetarian restaurant attached.

Finding and serving a genuine teacher is a powerful step on the path to self-understanding—someone who has been further along the path, who has learned by experience, can show you things you may never find on your own. The test of a genuine holy person is whether in that person's company you feel a greater awareness of divine presence. I felt this with my teacher.

When I was a young man I wanted answers and I needed guidance. In time I had to learn to live from my own inner guidance. If you have identified so completely with your guru, as I did as a young man, you will still have to find yourself. When my teacher left this world in 1977 I found that to follow an external guide was only the outer part of my journey. I also had to go inward. By then I was director of the London Radha Krishna temple, responsible for a diverse community. My first wife left me and emigrated to America. We had fulfilled our destiny together. I remarried and was blessed with a wonderful son and daughter. My wife and children became my teachers and inspiration.

I continued working for the community, but with a growing family I returned to the world and began earning a living by working for the environment. I needed to find my own way, to explore the natural world and discover myself as an individual spirit. When we are born into this world, we embark on a journey to find ourselves. Life, which begins simply, gets complicated. Attachment and loss, hope and hurt, success and failure, change us. The passing years softened my firm edges and wore me down. I was shaped by the river of time. Little by little I began to find myself.

FOLLOWING THE FLOW

In my late thirties, when I wanted to experience more of the world I had turned away from at twenty, I met Martin Palmer, a far-sighted man who became a close friend. Martin was doing amazing work bringing together the world's religions to conserve nature. Inspired and supported by him I went to India to research my first book, *Hinduism and Ecology*. I became a student of nature and people, and was moved to take up environmental activism.

In the pilgrimage town of Vrindavan, sacred to Krishna, I met local people and talked to them about their connection to nature. I learned about the growing separation between them and their fragile environment. In the shadow of nearby Delhi, a mega-city expanding at dizzying speed, their ancient settlement was assaulted by pressures of population, industrialisation, mechanised farming and escalating numbers of pilgrims.

One day as I sat on the bank of the River Yamuna I felt an immense sadness. Echoes of temple bells, gongs and calls of peacocks mixed with smoke from dung-fuelled fires to waft through the still air. On the far side of the river through the early morning mist I saw fields of grains, beyond them a small village shrouded in trees—a view barely changed since medieval times. Behind me was the town, crowded with temples, guest houses and markets, fifty thousand inhabitants and a similar number of pilgrims. I watched a black stream of sewage emerge from the town and ooze beside me down to the river ten feet below, where it joined the effluent from dozens of similar streams along the bank.

I had been learning how the river, on its way from the Himalayas four hundred miles north, passed through Delhi where it became an open sewer. Here, eighty miles downstream and partially cleansed by the water's turbulence and clarifying heat of the sun, it was again being poisoned. I contemplated what was happening to the harmony and balance of this ancient settlement. Once it had been nourished on three sides by its life-giving river; now it was surrounded by a toxic stream.

In subsequent years I travelled round India and saw at first hand how this story was repeated in every settlement. As the old wells and rain-harvesting ponds were replaced with piped water supplied by municipal water boards, sanitation couldn't keep pace with the expanding population and everywhere water-born diseases were rife.

My environmental work eventually took me to the 2003

World Water Forum in Japan, where I learned what a vast and complex task it is to ensure the long-term supply of clean water needed by the billions of humans on the planet. I met dedicated experts and humanitarians working to support people's basic needs, but I also learned how the world's water supplies are increasingly controlled by a handful of multi-national corporations, largely coordinated by the World Water Council based in Marseilles.

In the process these water companies are building ever-larger dams, irrigation infrastructures and water-treatment plants, all of which are transforming the traditional harmony and interdependence between people and water into a market-place of supply and demand with huge revenues at stake. Water, the sacred basis of life, has become a global industry.

KEEPING IN BALANCE

Since human culture began, water falling from the sky was received as a gift of God. A relationship was drawn between human behaviour and the bounty of the heavens. Some may now dismiss this as a superstition. I do not. I see the way we treat ourselves, one another and nature, as creating our own fortune. If collectively we act in a way that is harmful to the natural order, if we become a burden to the web of life of which we are a part, then we disturb nature's balance. This is visible in our changing climate.

The connection between human behaviour and climate was understood by ancient wisdom. To paraphrase the *Bhagavad Gita*, 'Humans depend on crops; crops depend on rainfall; rainfall depends on working in harmony with the divine.' In other words the way we treat ourselves, one another and the Earth are all related. Each depends on the other. We cannot treat nature in a destructive or wasteful way and expect harmony and abundance.

For two decades I worked with environmental issues in India and around the world. I saw nature's powers of creation and destruction. I saw how much humans are capable of damaging our environment, and met people dedicated to caring for nature and reversing the damage. I wrote books, my children grew and I became a grandfather. I had to admit my attempts to change the world had achieved little. I was called to learn all over again, to enter a period of inner transformation and renewal.

So I entered the next element, fire.

RIVER MEDITATION

You are on a grassy verge beside a quiet forest stream. Overhanging trees spread a cool shade.

Sit on the turf, feel its softness and warmth beneath you.

Watch the current, its ripples and eddies, the forest leaves and twigs carried along the surface, see the riverbed through the clear water.

Hear the water's gentle sounds.

See how the water follows the contours of the ground, flowing ever onward.

Notice how the flow is always there, how it occupies the space and fills it with life.

Feel the same spirit of life flowing inside you—peaceful, yet never ceasing.

Follow that flow wherever it takes you,

Be in that flow, let the flow be in you.

RAIN MEDITATION

Rain descends softly, first pattering on the roof, then as a downpour falling in waves. Leaves and ferns nod as they soak in the life-giving draught. Rivulets along the ground make puddles, streams trickle from gutters to fill garden tubs. Distant flashes of lightning spread a soft rumble across the sky. Birds take flight, mothers call their young.

Feel the same life-giving water flowing through you——as the fluid you drink soaks into your organs, cleansing and revitalising your body. Day and night this inner river nourishes and carries away impurities, emerging as a golden stream to soak once more back into the earth.

The sky which was dark brightens, light fills the air. The rain dwindles, leaving a fresh world, clean, dripping and shining.

OCEAN MEDITATION

Imagine you are sitting on a sandy beach at sunset.

As the sun sinks a golden light spreads over the sky and is reflected in the ocean.

Listen to the surf as the waves break on the shore and gently recede.

Bring your attention to the energy at your base, where you are supported by the warm sand.

Feel the energy rise to touch your sacral area, where it creates a fluid sensation.

Feel here the element of water, its ebb and flow in your sacral chakra, the sensation of movement.

Release old patterns of attachment and welcome the new experiences that life brings.

Feel your connection with oceans, rivers and life-giving rains.

Thank nature for her gift of water that keeps you cleansed and open to life's changes.

The Third Element

FIRE ❖ *Transformation*

On top of Fairfield Ridge in the blazing sun

ONE RARE SUNNY DAY IN THE LAKE DISTRICT I walked up the valley with my notes and writing paper, a bottle of water and a packed lunch. The sun shone brightly on the valley floor as I picked my way through clumps of turf and scrambled among stones. Following a path by the rushing stream, I planned to find a shady spot and stay out the whole day to work on my manuscript. There was not a breath of wind, and as the fells rose either side the temperature soared. By early afternoon I had reached the top of the valley, where no trees offered shade—only hillocks of turf and rock amid the bog. I realised I was in a heat trap and without my sunhat. Hot and thirsty, I cooled off in an icy pool, ate my provisions and finished the remains of my water.

My path ahead was blocked by the steep rise to Fairfield Ridge which closed off the head of the valley. I had intended to turn back, but my spirit of adventure sent me scrambling up the slope, angling for a distant outcrop on the ridge a thousand feet above. Three times on my way up I collapsed onto the stony slope to gasp for air and still my racing heart. At last I reached the top.

Around me opened a breathtaking panorama. As far as my eye could see were the peaks and humped backs of Lakeland hills rising above hidden valleys. But in the burning sun, without shade or water, I couldn't stop to enjoy the view; I was starting to feel heat exhaustion. Parched and weak, I followed the ridge as it raked downward through the haze back in the direction of Lake Windermere. Four hours later, sunburned and almost delirious, I reached the shelter of my cottage, where I gulped down litres of cold water and collapsed on my bed. For two days I felt depleted. This modest adventure gave me a sharp reminder of the strength of the sun's rays.

TRANSCENDENT LIGHT

The sun is our companion throughout life, our supreme manifestation of fire. We rise with the sun and rest when the sun goes down. When the sun shines our mood is lifted; we have a sense of transcendent benevolence shining on all regardless of individual destinies—we are all blessed. That at least is how it feels in England, where we are happy to see the sun, because the sky is usually obscured by clouds.

We have a finely balanced relationship with our life source. We must learn to be in the sun without getting burned. This dazzling light shines upon us, so bright that if we look into it we are blinded; a light that we are utterly dependent on, yet which we dare not look upon directly. If we are over-exposed to it, this light can even bring us death. This awareness is particularly strong in a hot country such as India, where the sun is still revered as a deity.

The sun was the great deity of the old religions. In India the sun-god was Surya, who orbited the earthly realms. His cosmic chariot is represented in stone at the thirteenth century Temple of the Sun in Konarak, Eastern India. There Surya traverses the heavens, his chariot set on enormous stone wheels and pulled by seven horses. The royal houses that once ruled Rajasthan claimed descent from the Sun. They still call themselves Suryavamsa, the dynasties descended from Surya, whose face to this day is their royal crest.

The power of the sun is invoked in the ancient Sanskrit verse called *Gayatri*, meditated upon at sunrise, noon and sunset to mark the passage of light and dark and the movements of earthly time. The mantra conceives the sun as the source of inspiration. Sunlight shows us the world, allows us to know what we are and where we are; it is a living force, the conscious presence of the sun. Without this luminous presence we know nothing, therefore *Gayatri* is the first of mantras:

om bhur bhuvah svaha tat savitur varenyam
bhargo devasya dhimahi diyo yo nah pracodayat

I meditate on the divine light of that radiant source
Who pervades the earth, space and heavens,
Inspiring my heart and mind.

At dawn in London I like to climb nearby Primrose Hill to watch the sunrise. On the summit I meditate on the *Gayatri* mantra, feeling the sun's daily re-emergence as a divine blessing. The rising sun lifts my heart and frees me from fear. As night's shadows dissolve and light spreads, I feel the love that inspires all creatures to awaken to a new day.

LIVING FIRE

The sun enters all life as fire, source of light and transformation. It is the warmth inside our bodies, the molten core inside the Earth, the spark, the lamp, the flame that cooks our food. In India fire has always been sacred, worshipped as the fire-god Agni, remembered in English words like 'ignite'.

As a child I lay on my stomach close to the fireplace and gazed for hours into the glowing coals. In the heart of the fire I saw another world, where iridescent colours played back and forth; logs changed from wood to living fire, flames licking round them as their colour turned to red, orange, yellow, white and blue. In the glow of fire I felt a transcendent presence. Still, whenever I sit with friends round a bonfire or beside a wood-burning stove, I feel the fire drawing us into its company, enveloping us like a comforting friend. At night in a field, in cold or damp, the presence of fire transforms the atmosphere. The flames create a welcoming space and an aura of familiarity. In the company of a fire I cannot feel lonely or depressed.

A home needs a fireplace. The old English word for fire-place is hearth, similar to the old English word heart. Both are the focus of human life. The fireplace holding the sacred element of fire is the centrepiece, the place for cooking, for warmth, for quiet reflection, for gathering in comfort and affection, the symbol of life, love and security, the spiritual heart of the family home.

As well as being a source of comfort, fire is the catalyst that turns substances from one state to another, spilling from inside the Earth as volcanic eruptions, steam and hot springs, reminding us that our planet is alive and changing at a deep and mysterious level. On the surface Earth appears stable, but in her depths she is in fiery motion, fusing new rock and thrusting it to the surface.

Fire shapes our material world with its transformational power. In the furnace iron becomes steel, transformed into tools, machines and buildings; sand is transformed into glass; oil and its derivatives become plastics. Together these materials shape our age. And at the end fire will reduce our bodies and all it creates to ashes and to earth.

THE HEAT OF INDIA

I experienced fire's transformative quality in the summer heat of India. I was 25 years old when I stepped off a plane into Bombay's stifling wall of heat. All that day on a series of connecting flights I crossed the continent from west to east, ending in Calcutta. Early the next morning I travelled inland by bus to the pilgrimage town of Mayapur. I had no capacity to handle the heat. I acted as if I were in England, crossing fields at noon with my head bare, drinking from the nearest pump or well. Within days I fell ill with heat-stroke and tummy bugs. I have always found the heat in India hard to cope with, but on that first visit I thought I would die. During subsequent visits I adapted to India's water and climate—I now find the heat healing; it draws the impurities from my body and cleanses me inside and out.

In north India the summer temperature regularly rises above 40 degrees centigrade; sometimes it even touches 50 degrees. Its effect is to slow me down, bringing my awareness to the place where I am. Each step becomes an effort, my vision turns inward. I shade my eyes from the dazzling light, cover my head, reduce my pace and preserve energy to last the day. Time slows down. Space and distances contract. The radius of my attention reduces. Everything shrinks in the heat. I do less, but with more awareness.

The sadhus don't move around much either. They are the wandering holy people of India, constant reminders of the life of the spirit. In the heat of the summer they stay inside their meditation huts, beneath trees or in caves. They practice harsh austerities, some of them: deep meditation, fasting, long hours in solitary prayer, lying prostrate in the dust murmuring mantras. This mood of austerity is not unique to the Hindu tradition, but it is strong among the sadhu community. In a milder manner it became an element in my practice, in so far as a person like me was capable of austerity. I am a child of the West, where we grow soft with creature comforts and lives of plenty; my nature is not to be austere. Yet in my ashram years I restricted my eating and sleeping, spent time in meditation, withstood the heat of India and the damp and cold of England, to work long hours in service. This was the practice throughout my adopted spiritual family, the disciples of my guru; we demanded from ourselves and one another a life of penance, suppressing our natural instincts and desires, imagining this was required on our spiritual paths. But I began to be aware, in the years after our guru left this world in 1977, as one by one my friends relaxed their strict vows, that there was only so far we could go with single-minded renunciation. As with many things in my life, I was forced to retreat. Not to utter defeat—that blessing came later—but it felt like failure. As things began to break down, the need arose within me for transformation. My penance, my self-control, my fire of sacrifice faded; but they had not been in vain. They brought me to the next phase of my journey.

INNER FLAME

By the time I learned to embrace my inner fire, I had spent so long looking outside myself for strength that when in the end I found it inside, it frightened me. Within our bodies the seat of fire is the region of the solar plexus. This inner fire, that maintains body temperature and fuels digestion, is called in Sanskrit *vaisvanara*, the inner flame that in yoga discipline is fanned by the indrawn breath. As the fire of digestion it consumes all that we eat. This solar region is where our power lies; from here we learn to direct it in a balanced way, and here we encounter the power of inner transformation.

This happened for me within weeks of my sixtieth birthday, a time of life when I might have resigned myself to a gentle passage into retirement. Instead, change came upon me as searing sunshine follows a summer storm. As I entered my fire, guided by my friend Jörgen, my emotions were a turmoil of fear, apprehension and confusion.

Once you enter the fire the first thing you notice is that it feels cool. This is because by entering the fire your nature has become molten like the fire. When I stepped inside, crossing my threshold of dread and insecurity, I handed myself over to the all-seeing eye of love and acceptance, and felt calm and overwhelming relief. That was when I realised that the very thing I feared most, my own inner self, was the place where I could find the comfort and love I had always sought.

Scientists who study the sun say that inside its fire is cool. Temperatures in the sun's corona reach a million degrees, but beneath the corona the surface of the sun is relatively much cooler, around five thousand degrees.

This is exactly how it felt to me when I found inside the fire of transformation the cool flames of love. I saw that I could live from my heart without fear. I could release all previous notions of what I should be or do and follow my innermost wishes without fear of being judged. If I lived from my heart, for the sake of my real self, I would reach others with love, and feel their love surrounding me. All this I heard from my inner voice. If I reached out to people to give them love, in whatever way I could, I would feel myself loved. I would be living in the light.

Without light, the background state of this world returns to darkness, symbolic of mystery. Our tiny sphere of understanding seems little more than a pin-point of light amid the darkness of space. We need light to dispel our darkness, day to dispel our night. Until sunlight falls upon our lives we cannot see the world as it is. In a deeper sense, until the inner light of inspiration expands within us, we cannot perceive ourselves as we are.

I have lain in darkness at night, unable to sleep as my mind fills with doubt and fear. At such times I know only one thing to do. Light a candle and pray. Silently I focus my attention on my heart and wait for inner light to come. If I am fortunate I find that light, and know the darkness holds no threat—it is filled with an invisible presence of love.

LIGHT IN THE DARKNESS

Fire in any form—a candle, an oil lamp, flames—brings the sacred into our lives and reminds us of the light of divine inspiration. It is hard to imagine how much it must have meant, in the days before electric light, to have light from a flame amid darkness.

What must our ancestors have felt when they first encountered this unpredictable force of nature which burned and spat? Once they learned its ways, fire became their friend and protector, the treasure that transformed their fortunes.

I once watched a ceremony in an Indian temple in the hours before dawn. A flaming lamp was offered before the sacred image allowing us all to see the face of the deity, then the lamp was carried among the worshippers to bless us with its light and warmth. At that moment a power cut threw the temple into darkness. The light cast by the lamp took on a new meaning. As it was taken round, each person shone momentarily in its golden aura, each face a mirror of the divine, an island of magic and mystery.

This magical experience made me wish for more power cuts. Electric light prevents us experiencing true darkness, or the magic of candlelight, or seeing clearly the heavenly bodies when they emerge each evening into the night sky. Before the advent in my part of the world of street lights and light pollution the human mind was fed constantly by the visible mysteries of deep space: the Milky Way, the constellations of stars, the movement of the planets; all these would have been an overwhelming nightly presence in our lives.

DANCE OF THE NIGHT SKY

At the end of each day nature makes her children sleep; the darkness heals and restores all daytime creatures. This is nature's way—the diurnal cycle of light and dark restores balance, allowing the body to recuperate and rest for a fresh day. I have always found the early morning hours, before sunrise and the activity of day, to be my best time for quiet contemplation and prayer, when I am able to contact the silent inner presence. With the light of a candle I can connect to the deep wellsprings of the spirit.

Once, when I was staying on retreat in India, I rose early in the darkness and I stepped outside to see the stars spread across the heavens in the crisp night. Looking up at the constellation of Orion I saw for the first time the complete form of the dancing figure, the three bright stars forming his belt, his bow held before him. I could see this because in the clarity of the night the faint stars that made up the rest of the constellation were clearly visible, revealing the rippling contours of the full cosmic figure. I turned back to my meditation cottage, and a couple of hours later came out again. Still darkness covered the sky. This time I saw that the figure of Orion had moved, danced across the sky, while the thin crescent of the waning moon had risen on the eastern horizon. During the next hour I watched as dawn tinged the sky. There came a magical moment when the moon hung luminous in the light of approaching day, glowing soft and warm, her globe distinctly visible as she merged into the golden dawn.

While travelling in the Himalayas I have had my breath taken away by the magnificence of night skies. Lying on a rooftop ten thousand feet above sea level, I have seen spread above me the quilt of sparkling stars, no patch of darkness visible anywhere, all pulsating with jewels of light; not individual sparks, but entire landscapes of varying brightness, clouds of galaxies from horizon to zenith set in the folds of the vast tapestry of undulating space. I have looked up in wonder, thinking how little awareness I have of this nightly display of magnificence when I am under England's clouded neon-flooded skies. If I saw every night what I saw at that moment, I thought, I would see differently the dance of life.

This nightly appearance of heavenly bodies is a reminder of the powers that exist beyond our normal vision. During daytime sunlight illuminates this world and obscures the stars; in the same way my absorption in visible nature blinds me to the mysteries that lie within it. No wonder the stars and planets, the study of their movements and the art of astrology played such an important role in human history.

THE CARBON CYCLE

One of Earth's mysteries is how the planet regulates her temperature by balancing the heat absorbed from the sun with the heat she releases back into space. The living relationship between Earth and Sun has sustained the conditions necessary for life on Earth for hundreds of millions of years.

Part of this balance is the carbon cycle, which is so complex and nuanced as to be beyond our full understanding. One of its complexities is visible in the way trees capture carbon from the air and store it in their timber, where it becomes potential fire. Timber used in an enlightened way can build and heat our homes and cook our food. But if it is harvested relentlessly to be traded as a commodity, the earth is denuded and her protective cover ripped away for short-term profit.

In distant times timber beds sank deep into the earth where they were compressed into carbon. So they became concentrated fire. This was one way Earth stored latent heat. Now the heat stored in that carbon is being released at a tremendous rate. Deposits from forests that took 40 million years to lay down, and were stored a further 300 million years as oil, gas and coal, are rapidly being used up.

Everywhere this release intensifies, supported by military force. Armies roam the globe to seize and control Earth's resources. Wars are fought to harvest her stored-up wealth at a pace never before seen. Rivers of oil, coal and minerals bleed from her wounds and are burned into the atmosphere. Billions of electric bulbs, illuminating cities and industries, are visible from space as veins of fire that blaze in the night across the dark side of the planet.

Some scientists propose technologies to rebalance the carbon cycle. Yet whatever adjustment is made, nature and the planet will respond in unpredictable ways, because their conscious energies are not under our control. We are a small part of nature. Our obvious need is to adapt to our environment, rather than adapt our environment to suit us. This approach sees nature as wise teacher rather than unconscious matter for manipulation.

COLLECTIVE KARMA

In a matter of two and a half centuries, human industries have burned a major part of those millions of years of carbon deposits and released them into the atmosphere. This destabilising of nature's cycle is bound to bring unseen repercussions, the tip of which are now being felt. The resulting catastrophic disruption of weather patterns will bring profound change.

You could call this karma, or you could call it nature's response to our actions. A society's level of carbon emissions is a good measure of its patterns of consumption of Earth's resources. If people take more than they put back, more carbon is emitted into the atmosphere than can be absorbed by Earth's natural systems, and the balance in the carbon cycle is upset. Over time this imbalance disrupts global weather patterns, as is becoming increasingly clear.

What we call climate change demonstrates the principle of karma on a grand scale. Karma works for individuals as each of us influences our reality by the choices we make in our lives, arising from our conscious intentions. Karma is also collective. Group consciousness produces a collective experience reflecting the character and intentions of the group, be it a community, a nation or the whole human race. Each of us shares in the whole because we are interconnected, and we are affected by the activities of even a minority among us. The relentless expansion of the carbon economy is burning up the planet's resources so as to fuel our collective way of life. This is a manifestation of mass consciousness. Although it may be directed by the activities of a few, its consequences are felt by all.

One of the features of karmic reaction in our lives is that the effect is seldom simultaneous with the action that caused it; the seed of an action takes time to mature. Life gives us endless examples of this principle of karma. For example, the choices of my youth have their consequences decades later. The present cycle of industrial carbon pollution and climate change is another example. In the short term it appears to bring advantages, but there is a time delay: the carbon which was burned into the atmosphere over the last century is only now taking effect. The delay between action and consequence, in all aspects of life, makes their connection harder to see.

EVOLUTION OF HUMAN CONSCIOUSNESS

Humanity has been in this industrial cycle driven by carbon-based fuels for nearly three centuries. During this time human population has quintupled. The precursor of change was the misleadingly-named Age of Enlightenment, which shifted human perception of nature from a relationship of reverence to one of exploitation. This shift is the inevitable outcome of a loss of sacred vision. However, it may yet have a redeeming side. I have learned in my own life that when a way of living isn't working, my tendency is to push it to an extreme and force a breakthrough. This is human nature, to intensify a pattern of behaviour to breaking point, where it collapses to make way for a new phase of evolution.

When I walked into the suffocating heat at the head of Rydal Valley I was faced with a dead end. Being human I found a way to climb out of it, and in the process learned something about myself and the world. This is what we seem to have been doing by pursuing the path of industrial development. We are forcing ourselves to the limit of physical exploitation of the planet's resources. In so doing we are preparing to evolve to a deeper understanding of ourselves, a broadening of human consciousness. This opening of our perception to higher dimensions will lead us to rediscover nature as sacred teacher, to enter deeper into her mysteries.

Climate change looks as if it will be a major catalyst in our evolution. It will usher in a shift in the balance of life on Earth. We will learn new ways of relating with nature, not just in our actions, more importantly in our consciousness—in how we understand our relationship with planet Earth. Thus fire will bring about profound transformation in the evolution of human consciousness.

Fire is child of the most subtle of the physical elements, air. No more than a fragile vapour that moves over the surface of the globe, the slender membrane of air, outermost of Earth's physical coverings, is all that keeps us from the vast emptiness of space.

I will now enter air's embrace.

FIRE MEDITATION

You are sitting with friends around the radiance of a wood fire. See the dancing flames pulsate with heat, their colours changing from red to orange, yellow, white and blue.

See into the heart of the fire. Feel it warming you. Feel the heat on your skin, the glow on your face.

Hear the sound of fire spitting and crackling. Smell the aroma of woodsmoke.

Notice how the fire lights up the faces around you, casting flickering shadows on their features.

Feel the fire's enveloping presence, friendship and strength.

Become aware of a connection, a flow of life-giving energy between you and the fire, between the fire outside and the fire within.

SUN MEDITATION

You are on top of a favourite hill, there to watch the sunrise. The predawn air, cold and misty, awaits the warmth and light of the coming day. The eastern sky pales and a glow heralds the rising sun. Birds begin to sing, their calls echo across the landscape. As the sun's orb breaks above the horizon, golden light dissolves the last shadows of night. Dreams sink back into the unconscious as another day of activity beckons. Welcome the sun's blessings of light and warmth. Feel the sun's energy arouse you. Let his limitless prowess inspire you with wisdom and love.

The Fourth Element

AIR ❖ *Freedom*

Overlooking Rydal Water on a windy day

THIS MIDSUMMER MORNING THE AIR HOLDS a soft haze. From the window of my stone cottage I see receding woods and dew-lapped pastures, tree-lined ridges sloping to distant Windermere Lake, hills fading to the horizon— all tinged with layers of misty blue. High above, a blanket of cloud, cotton wool smudged with grey, muffles the landscape. The air hangs damp and still. Not a leaf quivers.

Along invisible pathways between treetops, jackdaws, finches, blue tits and swallows dart on their ceaseless errands. The air embraces them all. They hover, ride the winds, cross oceans, rest in the sky—the wind is their home. By comparison we humans, with our machines to propel us through the skies, are clumsy and wasteful. Only when we glide from mountain sides, or float soundlessly beneath hot-air balloons to drift on airy currents across seas, forests and deserts, do we fly in harmony with nature. Then briefly we taste air's freedom.

Of the four physical elements, air is the finest, yet most essential to life. If air thins, as it does at high altitude, we lose energy and consciousness. Humans can live for weeks without food, for days without water, for hours without heat, but without air we cannot live for more than a few minutes. We depend on it utterly, yet air holds us in the softest of embraces, offering almost no resistance. It is the epitome of soft strength.

EVER-CHANGING EMBRACE

We experience air by its touch. Whereas earth is solid, water liquid and fire burning, air is invisible. Earth has smell, taste, form and texture; water has taste, form and texture; fire has form and texture; but air has only texture. Air caresses us, cools or warms us, brings us refreshment, moisture or dry heat. A sea breeze, a rain-laden summer wind, a fog rolling off the ocean, a gust of hot air, a damp autumn gale, a chill arctic blast; each brings its own sensation.

Aromas carried on the air heal our spirit. Here in the Lake District, at my cottage door orange blossoms are in bloom. Their evening perfume delights me when I walk by, healing me with honeyed scents of citrus and sunlight. The fresh smell of new-mown grass reminds me of earth, of my childhood when my father cut the lawn as I played in the garden or explored the apple orchard, where honey bees floated among the blossoms as I lay in the long grass and felt its rough stalks enclose me.

From the cottage garden I can walk into the woods where the smell of damp pines draws me along the valley. As I follow the path amid the hush of tall trees, moist pine needles and leaves fill the air with the rich scent of the forest floor.

Trees regulate the atmosphere with their breathing. This makes them our perfect companions, for humans and plants breathe in complementary ways—we inhale oxygen and exhale carbon dioxide while trees do the reverse. The soil that nourishes plants and organisms living in the earth also depends on air for its nitrogen and oxygen, essential for fertile soil and healthy plants.

LINK TO THE INVISIBLE

Among the ways we know air, breath is the most intimate. Breath is life itself. I remember fighting for breath during cross-country runs at school. In my teens I boarded with a community of Benedictine monks in a sprawling country house on a crest of the Sussex Weald. The school's stone turrets overlooked four hundred acres of woodland, streams and rolling pastures over which in winter our masters sent us out to run. We set off from the school in tight clusters soon strung out in a tortured file, slithering and trudging our way round a five mile circuit. We wove though dense woods and thickets of brambles, plunged into steep-sided muddy streams, traversed ploughed fields and climbed grassy hills, where we caught fleeting glimpses of the school lawns and terraces far away on the ridge. The test was not so much of my aching muscles and tired limbs; it was the struggle to breath. Could I inhale sufficient oxygen to drive my beating heart and failing legs? My lungs simply could not contain my need for air. By the time I staggered over the finish line, doubled over with stitches, I could only collapse headlong on the grass, arms splayed, gazing upward while I battled to fill my teenage lungs. As I caught my breath, air slowly stabilised my system, filled the gaps, eased the pain and exhaustion, and restored my life and energy.

While I was with the monks my father visited on rare occasions. I was making the transition to adulthood, and at last we became friends. Several times at school I had been beaten for smoking, which hurt my sensitivities terribly but in no way discouraged the habit. In my last year he came to a parents afternoon in the sixth form common room and astonished me by offering me a cigarette. Smoking for him was as much an act of defiance as for me, because his research was among the first to prove conclusively the link between smoking and lung cancer.

His concession to this discovery was to switch from cigarettes to a pipe. Smoking with my father in front of the monks felt to me like liberation. After that our friendship flourished, our conversations became honest and intimate. Three years later, with him on the verge of divorcing my mother, both of us about to leave home for good, we shared a bedroom and our deepest thoughts on our spiritual journeys and the meaning of life. Strange how of all things it was smoking that brought us together. Smoke inhabits the airways, damages the lungs, throat and heart, yet at the same time makes human beings more sociable creatures. Is this because, even while it reduces the oxygen to the brain, it focuses awareness on the act of breathing and on the shared smoke-filled space between smokers? I gave up cigarettes when I was twenty—I found a better way to connect with that inner space—but I still feel an empathy with those huddles of smokers exiled onto pavements everywhere.

It is not just oxygen that sustains us—our breath carries etheric energy, the life force that circulates in the body. In yoga this life force is called *prana*, an invisible presence essential to our lives and consciousness. Yoga tells us to observe the movement of breath, because air moving harmoniously through the body brings vitality and health.

BORNE BY BREATH

Life starts with our first inhalation as a baby, and ends with our last expiration. Anyone who has ever had the privilege to witness it knows what a mystery that last breath is; the irrevocable moment of separation that releases the spirit from the world of touch.

I sat with a lifelong friend who was slowly dying. His face was pale and bare like a bleached landscape, yet he shone soft and cool like a wild white rose. His breath came in shallow gasps, each one so difficult, so laboured, yet when the last breath came it was like a loving caress, the moment of release so longed for.

Two years later, as I embarked on writing this book, my mother reached the end of her eighty-seven years on Earth. I hurried overnight from the Lake District to be with her. All our lives we had struggled to know one another, to see through the fears that separated us, past our roles as mother and son to the person within. At the end we fulfilled our journey, unconscious lovers who at the moment of parting at last reveal their true feelings. When finally I told her from my heart that I loved her, that she was beautiful and blessed, she became radiant. As she struggled to breathe through those last hours, I beside her holding her hand, she seemed so helpless, so small and vulnerable.

When the end comes we have no choice other than to surrender to the hands of the unseen ones who cared for us all along. As the breath slowly drained from her I felt her do the same in one last long outpouring, and knew she was free, beyond the pain, the confusion, the fear of this place, safe in the arms of angels. In that moment I loved and was loved. I felt us both blessed beyond measure. I saw her room fill with light, the atmosphere instantly calm and saturated with peace.

In life, breath puts me in touch with myself, and in death it carries me onward. Breath does not have to be willed by me, it is willed for me. Rather than me breathing the air, the air breathes me. As I learn to observe my breath, to feel the passage of air through my nostrils and throat filling my lungs and departing again, I feel my life, I feel closer to myself and know I am part of the world. Without my having to command it my body knows to breathe, when to inhale, to exhale, and finally when to be still.

UNION AND SEPARATION

Air unites us but also pulls us apart. All creatures must breathe in and out, just as we must hold on but also learn to let go. Life leaves us no choice. This holding on and letting go, this dual rhythm, this keeping company and being separated, is with us all through life.

On high pressure days, when the air is motionless, I feel it holding me. A thin layer of cirrus clouds lingers high above, sound has a dreamy quality, the drone of a far away plane fades and swells, buzzing insects flit in and out of hearing. An atmosphere of peace spreads around me and sinks deep inside. Then my heart expands and I feel part of the expanse of air, joined with the web of life.

When atmospheric pressure drops the wind blows, and nature takes on a different face. To walk near woodland in an autumn gale, to see the trees whipped back and forth and hear their limbs creak, fills me with excitement. The wind tugs, the landscape heaves and sighs like a ship in stormy seas. Wind, bringer of change, cleanses the environment, clearing away the old to make way for the new.

In the autumn of 1987 a great storm swept through southern England. In the early hours before dawn a series of mighty gusts felled half the massive plane trees in Russell Square like matchsticks. I saw them stretched along the ground, a race of fallen giants, roots exposed to the sky. I felt bereft. Those mighty living things had watched over most of my adult life. They had seen the city wrap its noise and pollution about them; stood silent as children carved initials on their trunks and lovers caressed beneath their outstretched branches; witnessed my comings and goings for twenty years. Now it was their turn to go, ripped away by the wind.

REMEMBERING MY FATHER

Among the fallen plane trees I thought of how my father left. When I was small we used to stand together each morning on a tree stump in our garden, watching for the bus. We boarded together, and at the bottom of the long hill he got off to catch his train to London, leaving me in the care of Miss Woodward who taught me at kindergarten. Riding the bus with her to Crowborough I learned the Bible quotations displayed above the windows. One of them remains with me still.

Do not store your treasures upon earth, where moth and rust corrupt, and thieves break through and steal. Store your treasures in heaven, where neither moth nor rust corrupt, and where thieves do not break through nor steal; for where your treasure is, there will your heart be also.

Years later I stored my treasures in the temple that I helped build in Soho. When it was ready I invited my father to see what I had made. It was beautiful and I wanted to share it with him. He came, but he refused to set foot inside; it was after all the place that had taken his son from him. He could never bring himself to accept that I had chosen a different path to God, one that he disapproved of. The following year I went to see him. He was weak and irritable, and we argued. A chasm had opened between us, our lives had grown so far apart that we couldn't reach across. Then he revealed that he was in the final stages of cancer, the result of his years working with x-rays without protection in his laboratory. In the same breath he asked me to leave. I was distraught.

'We'll make up,' I said to him as we stood on his doorstep. I promised I would return in a few days.

'I would rather you didn't come back. I don't want to see you again.'

With those words ringing in my ears I left, shocked and confused, and hurried back to my service at the temple—I had many responsibilities to manage the community in those days. A week later my sister called to say he had died and the funeral would be on Wednesday.

I went to the big church in Kensington and stood among the mourners, feeling as if I wasn't there. I looked at the coffin and thought, he's not here either, just his bones. He was somewhere else. When the hearse left for the cemetery I stayed in the empty church. I was numb, confused by my lack of emotion. As I wandered through the aisles, I suddenly felt him with me. Light seemed to descend and the weight inside me dissolved. His voice spoke, 'You know, old chap (he used to call me that), there's no need to be upset. I am much happier now. A great burden has been lifted. From where I am you would be amazed to see how little all this matters, the worries and cares of life on earth. So please don't be sad. Remember I always loved you.' Then he was gone, and I was free.

Invisible air holds the power to crush us or release us, or both at once. Its invisibility teaches of all that is invisible. It marks the boundary of the visible and invisible worlds, the subtle place where they penetrate each other, where the physical powers of matter meet the subtle powers that energise them, where the realms of earth, fire and water meet the ethereal life beyond.

Air is our link to the finer elements, the ones we cannot see. I will now enter these as I move to the fifth element, ether.

MEDITATION—FEELING ONE WITH AIR

Sit comfortably, relax and close your eyes.

Observe your breath moving in and out, allowing it to deepen and lengthen in a way that comes naturally.

Feel the passage of air moving through your body.

Be aware that you are drawing air from the ocean of air that surrounds you and mingles inside you.

Feel the air gathering toxins from your body, whatever is not required, and carrying them away. Experience it entering your lungs and dispersing through your bloodstream, supplying oxygen throughout your body, leaving you refreshed and replenished.

With each exhalation feel yourself cleansed; with each inhalation feel yourself nourished.

Feel the ceaseless flow of air rinsing you clean.

Visualise the great expanse of air encircling the earth, nourishing and holding all creatures.

Feel yourself connected to all life in the embracing expanse of air.

The Fifth Element

ETHER ❖ *Inner Life*

The view from the top of Nab Scar

OVERLOOKING MY COTTAGE IS A STEEP FELL called Nab Scar. Near its summit, between two rocks, nature has provided a sitting place carpeted with turf, shaped like a large natural armchair. Here I can shelter from the wind and absorb the panoramic scene. To the south stretches Lake Windermere; before me across the valley is Loughrigg Fell; a thousand feet below is Rydal Water; beside it gentle Grasmere leads west up the valley toward Easedale and the road to Keswick. Each of these valleys, lakes and hills has its own history and flavour; its steep-sided dales, swift-flowing streams, waterfalls, lakes and woodland. And there is something else, an intangible presence that draws me, and thousands like me who come to the Lakes: an invisible presence in the ether.

Using our subtle senses we can perceive the presence and qualities of ether. We all have this capacity, but not all of us are aware of it. The element of ether is everywhere, and in some places it is more easily felt than in others. The tops of hills, the banks of rivers, beneath an ancient tree, a wilderness where nature has been allowed to flourish untamed and free from pollution——these places vibrate with etheric energy. Some places become sacred because enlightened souls lived there, pilgrims sanctified them with prayer, or they have been long revered: Glastonbury Tor in Somerset, Avebury Stone Circle in Wiltshire, or footpaths like Pilgrim's Way that carried pilgrims along the North Downs to Canterbury. Visitors feel the special quality in such places without needing to know why; they just feel good.

All these are locations where the ether carries a powerful healing effect on the mind. Sometimes an entire landscape may be endowed with a special energy, like this Lake District, the Vale of Avalon in Somerset, or the sacred land of Braj, home of Krishna in India. My local power point in London is the summit of Primrose Hill, set in parkland just north of the city centre, with panoramic views over Central London and beyond. It is a place to which Londoners are naturally drawn. When I am there in the early morning I feel the energies that radiate from the summit out across the city below. In my mind's eye I see a glowing latticework of pulsating channels spread in all directions, collecting the energy flows and the imprints of millions of lives, drawing them to this hilltop where they converge to meet the steady flow of healing energy drawn down from the sky. That at least is how I see it and what keeps bringing me there.

Our planet is wrapped in a web of etheric currents creating patterns of energy lines. These magnetic lines are associated with underground streams and aquifers. The ancient art of dousing can be used to locate energy flows and water sources, but even without this aid persons whose subtle senses are attuned can feel the flow of ether. The siting of sacred places or important habitations and meeting places seems to have responded, consciously or unconsciously, to energy lines in the landscape.

MYSTERY UNDERLYING LIFE

The fifth element, ether, is a mystery. In Sanskrit it is called *kha* or *akash*. Esoteric traditions have long known ether as the finest of the five great elements: earth, water, fire, air and ether. Unlike the elements so far, however, ether is not perceived by our physical senses or with conventional scientific instruments. Modern scientists have doubted its existence, but quantum physicists are finding ways to study it under such names as dark energy or quantum field theory.

I have always looked for the underlying pattern of life, the way that everything connects together. I know many of us have. It is apparent to me that the visible world of the senses is part of a greater reality. Within each of us is an interior universe of feelings, memories, inspirations, of loves and losses. Yet none of this is visible to our eyes, nor can it be more than dimly discerned with the help of scientific instruments. From this simple observation, I know that reality is infinitely grander than my physical senses are telling me.

DREAMS OF FLYING

My journey into this grander version of reality began early on. I remember as a boy of six or seven, alone in my attic bedroom lying in the darkness, I sometimes detached from my body and floated around the house. Usually I would go downstairs to be with my parents in the sitting room. Looking down on them from the ceiling I could hear their muffled voices but couldn't decipher their words. They couldn't see or hear me, and I saw the scene lit only by a dull flickering glow.

At other times, back in my bed, my body felt vast and distant; my hands and feet heavy and enlarged. Space couldn't be measured and I felt myself only as an awareness without dimension. In that hypnotic state I heard and saw rays of etheric light that seemed to emanate from faraway places. They passed through the room and through me, and connected me with somewhere beyond this life. These experiences made me feel peaceful and still, but they also unsettled me because I couldn't understand them. From about the age of eight they faded and I never spoke about them.

I left home for boarding school, to be a chorister at Westminster Cathedral. There I lived with fifty boys in a single large dormitory where we slept in double-tiered bunk beds. At night my heart would fill with an intense longing to be home. As I drifted off to sleep with this thought revolving in my mind I sometimes found myself high above London, and realised I could fly home. Because I didn't know the way I tried to follow the railway line from Victoria station. Sometimes I reached home, but usually I ended up getting lost and having wonderful dreams of flying, which I tried to repeat whenever I could.

These kinds of experiences, which I am sure are common among children though often forgotten, gave me a natural appreciation of the etheric body and the realms of ether, and prepared me to explore altered states of awareness in later life. I continued to have mystical and intuitive moments all through my life, right up to the present. My adventure of discovery goes on; each day brings a new insight, another revelation, a fresh chance to learn and deepen. This is why I am fascinated by the *Samkhya* vision of nature, because it includes four invisible elements, beginning with ether, that underlie the visible fabric of this world.

ETHER AS SPACE

Ether is the element in which the cosmos expands. It is particularly the medium for communication. Sound travels through ether, as do electromagnetic impulses passing through the apparent emptiness of space. What appears to be empty space throughout the cosmos is ether. Therefore another translation of the Sanskrit word *akash* is space, the element that holds other elements and gives access to mind.

This mysterious substance that pervades the universe is poetically described by Krishna in his secret teaching in the *Bhagavad Gita*: 'See how the mighty wind, blowing everywhere, moves always within the vastness of space *(akash)*. So all beings move in Me.' According to this teaching, air is suspended in ether, and ether itself is an extension of the all-pervading divine presence. The thin envelope of air that embraces the Earth is held in all-pervading ether.

Early scientists perceived the need for an encompassing material that enveloped the physical world and filled its empty spaces; but twentieth century physicists doubted its existence. The reason for this was simple: instruments made of earth, water, fire and air could not detect the element of ether. A system of physics that limited its investigations to the four elements of matter so far described in this book was bound to leave many phenomena unexplained. Quantum physicists now describe light and other impulses that behave sometimes as particles and sometimes as waves; they observe phenomena that defy conventional physics; they know things happen in the universe that they cannot explain. Many of these mysteries appear to be hidden in the element of ether, or space.

One of these mysteries is how planets, stars and galaxies remain in dynamic spatial relationships with one another across the reaches of space, as if connected by invisible channels of communication. Another puzzle is how electromagnetic waves travel over vast distances through the universe. The electromagnetic spectrum includes radio waves, microwaves, infrared radiation, visible light, ultraviolet light, x-rays and radioactive gamma rays, and other frequencies, no doubt, yet to be found with manmade instruments. The medium in which these waves move is ether.

SOUND VIBRATIONS

Sounds heard by the human ear are in the frequency range between 20 and 20,000 Hertz, and our voices create vibrations in the middle range of this this spectrum. Although we perceive these sounds in the elements of air, water and earth, their natural element is ether. One way to understand this is to consider the relationship between radio waves and sound. Radio waves exist all around us as vibrations in the ether, but we can't perceive them with our five senses. First they must be converted into sound waves by a radio receiver—then we can perceive them. In the same way, sounds transmitted in ether are relayed to our ears through the physical elements, primarily air.

There are many frequencies we humans don't hear, but which still affect us. Our voices carry ethereal vibrations. For example, truth has a vibration, and so does untruth; the vibration of love is different from the vibration of hate. Present in every person's voice is that person's energy, carrying higher or lower vibrations depending on the speaker's intentions. These vibrations may not be measured by electronic instruments, nonetheless they are present in the sounds we transmit. We hear these subtle vibrations, consciously or unconsciously, depending on how attuned we are to ethereal energy. Hence verbal communication is as much feeling and intention as literal spoken words.

Emotion is closely linked to sound, hence the voice carries emotion. An equally effective conveyer of emotion is music, with or without the human voice. Music creates an energetic field that can touch us in profound ways, reaching the core of our being. Music can evoke a memory laden with emotion or transport us to another time and place.

We all know how the presence of music can transform an experience. I may be in a stressful environment, yet the addition of calming music can change my mood so that I become calm. Film makers use music to add another dimension to the cinematic experience, to prompt emotions in their audience, to signal plot changes, and add colour and depth to their pictures and characters.

Sound vibrations made by bells, bowls, gongs, drums and rattles, as well as by the human voice, have the power to heal. Church bells suspended high in bell towers radiate healing sounds that unite a community with their place of worship and its rhythms. Sounds of nature, such as flowing water, the wind, birdsong, rainfall and thunder are wonderfully healing. They create a complete environment around us. The creative sound is called in Sanskrit *shabda*, and other traditions give it their own names such as the English word spell, meaning an incantation that carries creative power. When as children we wished to cast a spell, we used the word *abracadabra*, Arabic for 'make it so'. Ancient myths tell us how everything in this world was created through sound.

THE ASTRAL BODY

Just as we have physical bodies made of earth, water, fire and air, so we have astral bodies made of ether. The astral form encompasses the physical one. Under the right conditions it can be seen as an aura of soft light around the physical form. Favourable conditions for seeing it are in subdued light when the viewer and the one being viewed are both in a calm, expansive state of mind and a peaceful environment. The presence of the astral body can also be felt as magnetic energy. The aura extends a few inches beyond the body, and depending on the state of consciousness it may expand a good deal further. It is strongest around the hands, heart and temples. In rare cases it may be visible as a bright effulgence of light around a person of exceptional presence. If you ever experience such subtle perceptions, be thankful and trust them.

In the case of an awakened person, or one in the process of awakening, the astral body is active in a harmonious way; energy flowing freely, bringing feelings of well-being and vitality. One of the effects of regular yoga practice is to awaken and harmonise the ethereal body. The energy that flows in the ethereal body is called in Sanskrit *prana*. In Chinese tradition it is called *ch'i*.

As water assumes different states—frozen, liquid or vapourous—so we can experience ether as a dormant presence, a flowing energy, or a pervasive energetic field that connects one being to another and links us all in the web of life.

When emotions are suppressed in the ethereal body their energy is blocked, frozen like ice. Etheric energy in this frozen state becomes a knot of unresolved emotion bringing heaviness and immobility. These trapped emotions lodge in a particular region of the anatomy, where they can cause sickness. As we learn to recognise and feel these emotions they melt and begin to shift, returning us to vitality and good health. Psychotherapy and counselling aid this process; as do spiritual healing, prayer and meditation, and yoga practice.

In the next state, when the frozen emotions start to flow, movements of etheric energy induce feelings of wellbeing and joy. They are part of normal healthy living, but are mostly unrecognised or misunderstood by those who feel them. When I went through my inner changes I felt these movements intensely. Sometimes I had to stop and sit motionless, floating in a sea of inner sensation whose waves caressed my interior and my limbs. These waves held colour, and emotions like forgiveness and love. They filled me with inspiration and creative energy. A moment of such illumination was described by the poet W B Yeats:

My fiftieth year had come and gone,
I sat, a solitary man,
In a crowded London shop,
An open book and empty cup
On the marble table-top.
While on the street and shop I gazed

My body of a sudden blazed;
And twenty minutes more or less
It seemed, so great my happiness,
That I was bless'd and could bless.

When you regularly feel such things your whole life changes. Just to be alive is to be full of joy and light. The ordinary becomes extraordinary.

BREAKING THROUGH

The third way of experiencing ether, which is a natural outcome of inner energetic movement, brings integration. One of the great blessings to be experienced in life is an awakening of the vital etheric energies. This awakening brings a connection with all other elements through awareness of the etheric field that pervades everything, integrating the major elements—earth, water, fire and air—with the element of ether. Ether is the substance in which these other elements are united and balanced.

Something like this happened for me over a period of eighteen months following the moment of disintegration I described at the beginning of this book. It was accompanied by a release of stored up emotion, sometimes mild and gentle, at other times overwhelming. There were times when I doubted my sanity when exposed to a whole new set of sensations that revealed my life in a radically new perspective. Eventually the whole experience transformed my life.

When I first became intensely aware of my inner movements of ether I feared what was happening to me, but I now see that, far from pulling me away from reality, my experience made me more fully integrated and present.

The more I became aware of these subtle energies as a positive life-giving force within me, the more sensitive I became to the energies of those around me. I became more aware of their feelings and more able to respond intuitively to them. However, I realised that I must work on balancing my own energies, otherwise my energetic field could disperse and mix with others, draining my emotional wholeness. This happens to us all when we allow our feelings to become too entangled with those around us and lose our emotional integrity.

I began to realise how important emotions are to self-understanding. Ether, the home of emotion, is the subtle element that bridges the finer elements of mind, wisdom and ego with the physical elements of earth, water, fire and air. The etheric body is the link between the inner self and the outer body. It is a misunderstanding on the spiritual path to attempt to suppress or deny emotions. Feeling, exploring, allowing and expressing them, is an essential part of spiritual growth.

Any great influx of sensations will bring new ideas and inspirations. Along with these comes a completely fresh sense of what matters in life. This will be accompanied by feelings of emptiness and loss as old attachments fall away. Assailed with these unfamiliar sensations and perceptions, and the possibility of radical transformation, the mind may fill with fear and acute distress. When this happened to me it felt like a breakdown—indeed it was a breakdown of old ways of being.

One night I was enveloped in a fiendish black cloud of despair. I felt utterly blank, suspended in nothingness. I had to seek help so I sat in my meditation space. I began to feel some calmness, but I couldn't stop my tears. I visualised being surrounded with light. Still I felt so alone. I opened up my copy of *Dark Night of the Soul*, the sixteenth century book of Saint John of the Cross, and my page marker led me to this passage: 'The soul suffers terrible pain, like hanging in mid-air unable to breathe.' This was how I felt. The text said that God is purging the soul and such an episode cannot last long—if it did the soul would be over-whelmed. I felt a glimmer of encouragement. True enough the darkness turned to light and somehow I was able to function.

One response in the midst of such a mental crisis would be to seek therapy or medication in order to restore 'normality', the old familiar way of being. But this retreat from an imagined fear misses a wonderful opportunity to enter an expanded level of consciousness. Responding positively to such an opportunity and challenge, trusting in the present moment, allows growth, emotional and spiritual, to awaken more and more.

An opportunity like this may be triggered by a time of crisis, when living becomes filled with doubt, uncertainty and fear. At such a time the self cries out for inner change. Change always involves letting go of attachments. It is frightening to abandon familiar ways of behaviour that in the past brought a sense of safety and security. However, when the intense difficulty of life as it is outweighs the fear of change—then is the time for spiritual renewal and transformation.

ETHERIC PATTERNS

Strong emotions leave imprints in the ether. Hence a place has an emotional presence associated with the dramas it has witnessed. This imprint carries karma. The Sanskrit word karma simply means action, but in English usage it has come to incorporate the understanding that action brings a reaction. This karmic reaction creates an energetic pattern in the ether, a potential energy that influences the behaviour and emotions of those it touches.

Actions create an imprint because all actions begin as intentions in the mind. The quality of the intention gives substance to the action, and its memory is held in the ether. Energetic imprints are stored in the ether of places where prayer or sacred music have vibrated; where meditation has been practised; where love and harmonious relations have radiated; and places of care and healing. On the other hand places where human struggle has been enacted; where conflict has occurred; scenes of injustice or places where there has been great pain or unhappiness—all these places carry the equivalent energies. Great cities are filled with a vortex of karmic vibrations, yet each locality, each street corner, each home or garden within the city has its own karmic impression. Even a single room can carry a clear karmic imprint which is either disturbing or calming to those within it. Psychics read these etheric impressions and tell much about the history of a place by sensing its energies. A power point like an ancient country church brings peace and inspiration, whereas a hospital waiting room holds anxiety and fear, and a slaughterhouse carries trauma and violence.

CREATING HARMONY

Places of worship set aside for prayer and contemplation, for turning the mind to the finer qualities of life and to deeper awareness, carry powerful healing and pacifying influences. Sacred architecture reinforces this effect. Stone circles and standing stones channel and focus the geomagnetic energies of the landscape; domes magnify the vibrations they enclose; spires connect the sky and earth energies; entranceways and vestibules draw in positive energies and inhibit the ingress of negative energies; cloisters enclose a sacred garden or meditation space; an arched nave directs prayerful energy to the focal place of worship. These are all external to the inner life, where the true worship takes place, but they enhance it.

After I entered the experience of emptiness, I found comfort in a meditation circle in the heart of Camden Market in London. The market was an intense vortex of human interaction, full of chaotic energies. Yet the upstairs room where the circle met was an oasis of calm and light. The regular meditation practice created a sacred space and allowed me access to the temple of my heart, home of the inner guiding spirit. I will explore this inner temple when I come to the chapter on wisdom.

Since intentions create etheric vibrations, no activity is without subtle consequence. This is as true for individual lives and locations, as it is for communities, cities and entire countries. The energy created by a harmonious way of life creates more harmony, whereas a way of life based on exploitation, greed or violence recreates the same. Intentions pass from subtle thought to physical actions. In this way karma is transmitted.

Intentions form within the mind, and from there they are carried through the ether to the world of physical matter. From this we can see how, quite literally, mind shapes the world we live in.

Now, therefore, I will turn my attention to the sixth element, mind.

MEDITATION——ETHER

Sit in silence and close your eyes.

Feel the energetic presence within your body.

Beginning with the tips of your toes, your feet and lower legs, move your attention to each of your limbs in turn.

You may feel a lightness, a tingling in your limbs—perhaps a swirling or pulsing of energy.

Feel how energy flows through the centre of your body—your sacrum, stomach and heart; your throat and forehead.

Find which part you feel most drawn to and focus on that place.

What emotion does it carry—is it light or dark, dense or subtle, static or dynamic, contracting or expanding? Does it have colour?

Allow this energy to disperse into the space around you, to fill that space. Be aware how your etheric body is one with all space—with the ether spread everywhere. You are connected with all that is.

The Sixth Element

MIND ❖ *Self-understanding*

The moon above Rydal Water

EARLY THIS MORNING THE FULL MOON BLESSED ME when I woke to its rays streaming through my window. I dressed and walked out into the night. While the moon slipped in and out of the clouds, casting crisp shadows onto my path, I climbed the side of the fell. Halfway up its steep rocky slope I reached a smooth stone where I sat to contemplate the peace and solemnity of the moonlit night. Beneath me, dark and brooding fells floated in a luminous sea of mist that spread along the valley floor.

I closed my eyes and counted silently the rhythmic sound of my mantra on my beads. In the distance I heard the muffled roar of waterfalls, while inside the mantra rose and fell with my breathing and the beating of my heart, its vibration leading me deep. The silent moon spread across the landscape while the silent vibration of sacred names spread through the landscape of my mind.

So subtle and profound is the mind that it can hold within it the solid weight of hills, cold slabs of stone, soft silhouettes of trees, the distant sound of water, vaporous blankets of mist, drifting clouds beneath a silver moon— and envelope all these with the reverberating sound of mantra.

As the moon illuminates the land, so my mind captures the world and holds it within. What an amazing thing is mind!

THE MEETING PLACE

Mind is where my ego meets the universal presence manifest everywhere around me, where I form my unique experience of this world and my intimate connection with its source. Reality may be external to me, but I see and hear it within my mind, which assembles the impressions of my senses into its own version of the outer world. It is not possible for me to know what nature is; only what I think it is. If I want to change my experience of life, I must change the way my mind perceives life.

A friend told me a story of the power of mind. He visited Beirut in the 1980s at the outbreak of the Lebanese war. He was arrested at the border on suspicion of being a spy and held for one month in a cell too small to lie down in, kept under constant surveillance through the grill that formed the door to his cell, and fed on bread and water. Outside his cell he regularly heard executions. He had no idea what his fate would be since he and his captors spoke different languages. By good fortune he had lived for years in yoga ashrams where he learned to meditate and practice devotional exercises. So in his cell he spent all his waking hours absorbed in spiritual practice; he created an inner world where he meditated, visited temples, cooked sacred meals, sang, chanted and even taught. After a month, without warning, he was driven to the airport, handed his passport and put on a plane home unharmed. He told me that this month of solitary confinement, during which he was in more or less constant meditation, was the best experience of his life. This is the power of the mind.

During the life-changing psychedelic experiences of my youth, I saw a version of reality very different from the one I normally saw. Solid objects were alive with colour and movement, everything was filled with consciousness. I felt united with the world around me, swimming in an ocean of light, colour and love. This altered vision happens when we see the world without preconceptions. At times in meditation I have had similar experiences of unity and love.

Clearly my mental state influences profoundly the way I see reality. When I turn my mind to God I see nature as divine energy, filled with a presence of wisdom and love. In such a condition it is possible to feel deep inner satisfaction even in the midst of difficulties.

THE PEACEFUL MIND

Mind is the pivotal element on the journey to self-understanding, crucial to the inward journey, because it reveals who I am. A mind clear and open acts as a friend to the self. It is a pool of comfort and peace in which to be immersed and refreshed.

When the mind is confused and clouded with emotion, carried away by the stream of impressions from other restless minds, by news, gossip and entertainment, it fills with latent anxiety and becomes a screen to hide the inner self. The mental pool, agitated like a wind-tossed ocean, fills with waves of regret and currents of desire. With a mind in this state it is hard to find peace. Even in the midst of calm and plenty I feel miserable. For this reason my mind can be either my friend or my enemy.

The state of my mind is influenced by my companions, experiences and environments. I may feel that life doesn't offer me the right opportunities, but in any situation life offers choices, even small ones. The way I exercise my small choices influences the larger outcome.

An important principle here is the choice between instant gratification and longer term satisfaction. My mind wants instant enjoyment. It doesn't want to wait. The challenge is to train my mind to be patient and do the work. This is an abiding feature of all spiritual paths—some sacrifice is necessary to get the result. The whole journey of life teaches that I do not have to constantly strive for the things I don't have. If I am patient I will find the greatest riches and rewards of life are available to me in ways I could never have foreseen.

My own life has taught me this. I have never had much money, but I have received priceless gifts: a network of friends who inspire me, wonderful children and grandchildren, opportunities to travel and to work with remarkable people around the world. Life has given and taken in equal measure and I am glad for it all.

A silent mind invites inspiration to arise. An empty mind is therefore a blessed thing, because it soon fills with warmth and light. This is why the experience of emptiness is not the desolate thing it may sound. Emptiness turns to light. The underlying joy and love of the spirit filter through when the mind is clear. Then my mind becomes a gift bringing me inspiration and joy. To this end, the best advice I can give anyone is to develop or maintain a meditation practice, a regular time and space to allow the mind to be still.

The element of mind, as well as manifesting within each of us as a discreet mind-entity, is spread everywhere. The collective mental energy that spreads through time and space is like a group mind that has a powerful influence on our world and on each of us. None of us is immune from its pull. That is why our choice of companions is crucial. We can seek the truthful or the untruthful. To live in truth means to live in awareness of who I am; to be honest about myself to others and to myself; to find others who live in honesty.

BE A FRIEND

An aware person is friendly toward everyone, even to animals. This is well expressed in the Sanskrit mantra, *loka samastha sukhino bhavantu*, 'May all beings be happy and at peace.' How do I reconcile my aspiration to be friendly toward everyone with the need to choose my company with care—will I not have a tendency to judge another person before accepting their company?

I once knew a priest who had served his congregation for thirty-five years. He helped me answer this question. One evening I met him outside his church, blessing each member of his congregation as they left. I waited until he had finished, then asked him how he had managed to dedicate himself to their welfare for so long. I have never forgotten his answer.

'Inner life!' he said without hesitation. 'Unless you learn to love yourself, how can you love anyone else?'

How can I be friendly with everyone? I must make friends with myself. This means to cultivate my inner life, to see myself honestly and be aware of my faults, yet still accept myself as I am with love. Self-awareness is knowing I am not my mind, that I am something much deeper than my changing moods and attachments. The more I am inspired to live in self-awareness, the more I can share that inspiration with others, just by being open and friendly. In order to serve the world I must know and love myself, then I can be a friend to whomever I meet. I can be open and friendly to all, and with my intimate friends I can open my heart.

KNOW YOURSELF

One way to clear the mind is to harness it to inner wisdom. Without the inner direction of wisdom, bringing illumination and well-being, the mind is easily carried away by the senses, so that I end up being pulled this way and that. I can nourish my inner connection through regular practice such as meditation, mantra, yoga, prayer, spiritual reading and service—all with the help of uplifting company.

When I was young I made this choice. I was inspired by the teachings and practices of the Krishna people, so I joined their company. With them I spent my twenties and thirties cultivating self-awareness and teaching my chosen spiritual path to others. By immersing myself in spiritual life I learned much about the ways of the world, and about myself.

There was, however, a drawback. I found myself judging others, thinking my path superior to theirs. The nature of judgement is that it goes two ways—inward as well as outward. As well as judging others, I spent a lot of energy judging myself. I suppressed those parts of my mind that I didn't approve of, and this meant they hid deeper inside. In time this created conflict in my mind. These are common mistakes. Since none of us are ever going to be perfect, sooner or later we must learn self-acceptance. As I learned to accept myself I also began to accept others. I opened my vision to include other people's versions of truth. This is a continuing journey; there is always more to learn on the journey of self-understanding.

THE PRESENCE OF LOVE

Desire, attraction and attachment are part of the mind's nature. When we see the complexities of this world without awareness of the deeper presence within, we start to feel anxious and without peace. This is the common condition of most of us living here: nothing makes sense. The deeper presence we are missing is the presence of love.

The restless mind seeks pleasure and power, success and wealth. We are really looking for love, but we look in the wrong places. We confuse pleasure and power with love. We hold onto sensory pleasures and our sense of importance and use them to fill the empty space inside. Sooner or later we will learn that the feeling of emptiness, far from being a terrible thing, is a gift that leads us to the very thing we are looking for, to stillness.

In moments of quiet we find that the mind holds positive desires arising from deep within, inspiring us to seek understanding and peace. These desires are fed by wisdom. The more we hear and nourish these the less room there is for the rest. Since mind is the energy that makes the reality around us, mind is capable of making our lives hell, or it can make our lives heaven. We each have that power within us.

Just as we carry our personal intentions, so the universe carries a cosmic intention. The universal intention is to heal all who come here. The divine presence, the One who is the source of all life, wants only for us to find happiness.

'Your happiness is my happiness,' says that divine One. 'I am gentle, I am patient, I let you play, and watch over you always. Nature is my gift for you to use as you wish. She is magical. She heals you in just the way you need, and brings you back to me.'

SACRED SOUND

Healing begins in the mind. A powerful remedy to heal and illuminate the mind—and in my experience the easiest and most direct—is sound vibration carrying sacred intention. Sound penetrates everything. Sacred sound enters the physical world, bringing health and well-being to all who hear it; and moves inward to pacify and heal the mind, to inspire wisdom and soothe the ego.

Any sound created with healing intention carries healing potency. Of all sounds, mantra has the most powerful clarifying affect on the mind. A mantra is a collection of words or sounds intended to connect us to the deeper reality. The Sanskrit word mantra means 'free the mind.' Mantra does this by amplifying the divine presence. For example, the mantra *Om*, or *A-u-m*, is the sound form of the Supreme Reality; the mantra *Alleluia*, which contains the sacred name *Yah*, means 'praise God.' As a young man I was given the mantra *Hare Krishna Hare Krishna Krishna Krishna Hare Hare, Hare Rama Hare Rama Rama Rama Hare Hare*, which weaves names of God and Goddess into a song of love.

Mantra can be sung aloud, softly chanted to oneself, or repeated silently in the mind. Sound vibrates through the ether before it manifests as audible sound. A form of mantra meditation is therefore to contemplate the name of God silently, as for example, Saint Francis often did when he prayed, *Dio mio e mio tutto,* 'my God and my all.'

Audible mantra has the advantage that it more easily holds the attention. Singing sacred chants in the company of others is a spiritual practice found in almost every tradition. It draws upon the power of healing sound with the added benefit of being in the company of the awakened. When these two are brought together their combination is profoundly healing.

HEALING MEDITATION

As the mind fills with external impressions it becomes charged with restless energy. Meditation helps to heal this stored up tension because it puts you in touch with the unconscious mind, or deeper still with your inner wisdom. On the path of spiritual practice, regular meditation is the essential way to heal and harmonise accumulated energy in the mind, to keep the mind calm and clear.

When we practice meditation we inevitably encounter the seemingly endless chatter of the mind. This can be a discouraging experience. Do not be put off. In time and with regular practice the chatter will subside. When the mind is calmed, like still water, the distractions it carries settle and it becomes transparent. This allows you to see clearly the roots of your attachments and the sources of your pain. Once you see them, understand and accept them, they no longer have the same power over you.

One way into meditation is with mantra, holding the repeated sound of sacred words in the mind, chanting them softly or silently to yourself. Another way is to concentrate on your breath. A powerful practice combines both, harmonising breath and sound. For example, with your inward breath mentally chant Hare, and with your outward breath mentally chant Rama. There are endless variations and mantras, and no one way is correct or incorrect. Mantra meditation is an individual practice: find what works for you, the divine names or mantras that inspire you.

With regular meditation or mantra chanting, the senses become stilled and the mind starts to clear. Then meditation moves deeper and inner life is awakened. A great aid to developing inner life is yoga practice.

YOGA: THE OUTER PRACTICE

The system of yoga taught in India two thousand years ago by Patanjali is the most recognises form of yoga practised in the West. He divided yoga into eight limbs. The first four limbs relate to the outer physical body and the second four to inner life. Their aim is to balance the inner and outer, bringing our lives into harmony so that our inward and outward existence are integrated with one other, and ultimately with the source of all. This state of harmonious living is one meaning of the word yoga.

The first and second limbs of Patanjali's yoga system are

abstinences *(yama)* and observances *(niyama)*. Abstinences are nonviolence, truthfulness, non-stealing, sexual restraint and non-attachment. Observances are cleanliness, contentment, austerity, spiritual study and devotion to God. Taken together, these first two limbs of yoga add up to conscious living with a growing awareness of divine presence.

The third and fourth limbs are posture *(asana)* and breath restraint *(pranayama)*. Through combining exercise of the physical body with a deepening connection to the breath we learn to inhabit the body with growing self-awareness. Physical practice builds a strong and flexible body which is a great aid to mental clarity. Breath restraint develops awareness of the movements of inhalation and exhalation and the energy they carry. This energy is called *prana*, subtle life force. Awareness of the breath, allowing the breathing to deepen in a natural way without forcing it, calms the mind and leads the attention inward, preparing the way for meditation.

THE INNER PRACTICE

The fifth limb of yoga is withdrawal from the senses *(pratyahara)*. Here begins the practice of meditation. In this stage, with the mind calmed through breath control, we become increasingly aware of our inner life and the movements of life force within the body.

Heightened awareness of etheric energies that comes with yoga practice opens a world of experience and understanding, bringing gifts of inner vision and increased psychic awareness. Pursued for their own sake they are a distraction from self-understanding, but when accepted with gratitude they bring us closer to ourselves and to all of life.

The sixth, seventh and eighth limbs of yoga enter the realms of mind, wisdom and ego. They are sitting in concentration *(dharana)*; when the concentration becomes unbroken, meditation *(dhyana)*; and, as inner perception develops, complete absorption *(samadhi)*, in which the ego turns from its identification with matter to enter full communion with the Source of All in the temple of the heart.

DEVOTION

To enter these final stages of the eightfold journey of yoga, as laid out thousands of years ago by Patanjali, is difficult in this age because we are surrounded by the distractions of modern life. However the *Bhagavad Gita*, the great synthesis of yoga taught by Krishna in ancient times, offers a broad approach with a practical path for everyone. It includes *karma yoga*, the way of selfless service; *jnana yoga*, the way of wisdom; and *bhakti yoga*, the way of devotion.

A focus for the mind is a great help, not only for practising yoga, but for all of life. Devotion, part of Patanjali's second limb of yoga, gives the mind this clear focus. To still the mind we need something positive to focus on. The mind attracted to what is real abandons what is false; a space filled with light has no room for darkness. The practice of devotion takes positive steps to fill the mind with the truthful, while emptying the mind of the false. Both needs are there—to let go of what misleads and to embrace what inspires.

When the mind is stilled it seeks God as surely as a compass needle seeks North. The essential teaching of the *Bhagavad Gita* is that when an awareness of the presence of God is brought into all that I do, my mind finds a resting place of peace and love that brings lasting fulfilment. A natural unity and wholeness enters my life. This is called *bhakti*, devotion. *Bhakti yoga* is a complete path in itself, in which all of life, work and play, is dedicated in loving service to God.

Each of us has our own nature, and we will find a path that works for us. You may be drawn to active service, to meditation, or to devotion, or to a combination of these. The inspiration for your devotion may be the inconceivable divine presence; or the personal presence of God or Goddess. In all cases an inspired teacher or saint who has illuminated the spiritual path is a great help to attaining devotion. All these are included in the yoga path, and all can bring the gift of peace and healing to the mind. If you are supremely fortunate you will receive the priceless gift of inner divine presence, the experience of God's love embracing you within. This will become your constant source of inspiration and devotion.

We all seek beauty, love and wisdom. These are found in abundance in the mantras, teachings, sounds and images that are the treasures at the heart of the world's religions. The search for devotion is the essence of religion.

THE FOUR PROMISES OF RELIGION

Over thousands of years, teachings of inspired saints came to form the core of the world's religions. These teachings benefitted ordinary people. Although the great religions are losing favour in the modern world and are beset with problems, they survive because they continue to fulfil basic human needs. At their heart are profound truths and practices proven to work. Four essential benefits offered by religion in its many forms are: relief, reward, meaning and love.

I. RELIEF

Life is painful, and religion is a major provider of pain relief. While external pain can somehow be tolerated, pain in the mind makes life unbearable. We try to avoid it through all sorts of distractions—but it doesn't diminish because pain serves a good purpose. It urges us to grow and become more self-aware. If instead of turning away from it we listen to it, asking why it is there, we can be healed.

For many people the healing starts with religion. In times of suffering they put their faith in a power greater than themselves, and feel comfort. They stop battling to control the sources of their pain. Instead they change their relationship with life, from one of trying to change the world to one of allowing the world to change them. By avoiding harmful acts, learning to care for themselves and others, and joining in prayer and worship, they change the way they experience life. They learn to trust in a benevolent higher power. This is one way religion brings benefit to millions.

2. REWARD

A life ordered by religious faith not only gives relief; it also offers rewards. The faithful expand their sense of moral responsibility, become good citizens, gain friendships and the support of a community: they reap rewards here on Earth, and are promised more in the future.

However, though such rewards and promises are powerful motivators, they depend on obedience and good behaviour; hence they give rise to fear. The faithful are offered the hope of heaven; but also the fear of hell. Religion motivated by reward and punishment has a powerful hold over large sections of humanity. Its companions are sectarianism, prejudice, guilt, hypocrisy and condemnation.

3. MEANING

The safeguard to keep religion from fanaticism and intolerance is philosophy. Those who have solved their immediate needs want answers to the great questions of life such as: 'Who am I?' 'Why do I suffer?' 'What is the purpose of life?' In search of answers they examine the beliefs they have acquired. They notice that different religions give different answers, each claiming to offer the truth. We want universal answers to our existential questions. In this stage we delve into philosophy. We reject blind faith in favour of personal discovery. In the process we may doubt the idea of an external God altogether, if that allows us to go deeper into our search for truth. Eventually, if we enquire into who we are and what life is, we discover a common thread in all the world's religions. We cease to discriminate between one religion and another. We begin to realise the universal presence of the God within us all. This experience transcends sectarian beliefs and unites all paths.

4. Love

When inner life awakens, we discover love. In the end, love is the ultimate gift of religion. Once we find love all our other needs are met: they existed only to bring us to love. This is the irony: Jesus wasn't a Christian and Buddha wasn't a Buddhist. They were beings filled with love. Their followers were drawn to that love, and tried to hold onto it in the religions they perpetuated. But love cannot be confined in churches and temples, in rituals, books or doctrines. Love is found in the heart of every being, and in the divine Source of All. When we discover love we cease to need relief from pain, or rewards, or answers for everything—we live in acceptance of God's love, in trust that whatever comes to us is an expression of that infinite love. At this stage religion is no longer a search for relief, reward or meaning; it is an act of selfless giving and receiving.

Gods and Religions

Now we can see why belief in God can be so diverse: at each stage God means something different. In the first stage God is saviour, then God is justice, then God is truth, and finally God is love. God includes all these things. The reason people disagree about religion is because we each look for something different, and we find the image we seek. This is part of the mystery: we are individuals and we perceive in individual ways.

All four of these stages are present in mature religion of any tradition, since each one meets a profound human need. In consequence the world of religions is a bewildering mixture—we find people with every shade and combination of understanding and behaviour. Some are satisfied just to have found relief from their pain; some live in hope of reward and in fear of punishment; some think they have found answers for everything;—and a few radiate unconditional love.

I use the word religion in the broadest sense to cover all forms of shared faith, including yoga and contemporary spirituality, which show many of the characteristics of religion. In the end, religion and shared belief are inseparable from the human condition.

It is important to add that these stages of religion are not exclusive of one another, nor need they be in competition. In my own life I have experienced all these shades of faith. Each time I break through to a deeper level of experience, I feel I have understood something more. And each time this happens I know there is more to come and more to learn. My journey goes on—this book is part of it.

The Deeper Lessons of Religion

Religion that portrays God's love as conditional, saying that in exchange for obedience to a set of rules we will be granted God's forgiveness and acceptance, cannot bring the love and acceptance it promises. This kind of salvation is really a substitute for our own profound need for self-acceptance and self-forgiveness. We crave acceptance from others because we have not found it within ourselves.

God is pure unconditional love and acceptance. No condition is required, no rules need be obeyed to receive this complete love we all desire. It is only we who find ourselves unacceptable. We say, 'Who am I that I should be loved?' The answer is, I am a child of God. Because of my feelings of self-doubt and shame, I believe I am unlovable. I feel myself unable to accept the unlimited love that surrounds me. Yet that love is mine as soon as I open myself to receive it.

Let's say our search for happiness leads us to religion or a path of self-awareness like yoga. Through spiritual development we find comfort, inspiration, peace and a sense of fulfilment. Now that we have found our true purpose, we believe the fears that dogged our progress in life are over, our emotional wounds healed and our doubts resolved. But all too often those fears, wounds and doubts remain buried deep in the psyche. Unconsciously we carry our handicaps, emotional dependencies and addictions into our spiritual journeys. To begin with they hide beneath the surface. But, when we have learned enough to face our fears and look at them with honesty, they will return to conscious awareness.

OPENING A DOOR

This moment may feel like a spiritual crisis. The realisation that I have not progressed as far as I had hoped, that I still carry fears and attachments, may feel like failure, but actually it is a stage on my path to deeper growth. This is a time to be open, to be willing to learn and to accept help. As soon as we ask for help it will certainly arrive. Our apparent failure will open doors to greater insight, leading us to a deeper level of understanding. We will be guided to persons or experiences along our spiritual journeys that have important things to teach us. None of this comes by accident when the mind is open to seek self-understanding.

Sooner or later in the course of a lifetime we are given such opportunities that help us explore the hidden depths of our minds. The fears that held us back dissolve in the light of experience, and meditation gives us access to the wisdom of the unconscious mind. As the mind is stilled it becomes a transparent conduit to reveal deeper levels of consciousness where the wisdom of the self illuminates and heals.

MY PERSONAL JOURNEY

I have walked this road myself. I know what it's like to feel my supposed spiritual progress evaporate. As a young man of twenty I stepped out of conventional life to promise obedience to my guru and fill my days with service. Within a short time I felt my old self fall away, and found a new sense of completeness and clarity. I felt released from the ordinary course of events.

In time, however, my clarity and completeness became less certain. I discovered emotional and mental weaknesses, old attachments I had been unaware of. I saw my failings more clearly. My determination wavered and doubts arose. This is normal. My father was a wise man; before he died, he counselled me that in middle age I would have doubts; everyone does, he said, even saints and mystics. When it happens to you don't worry, he assured me, in time you will find your faith again.

What he didn't say, and which I now know, is that the faith you find will be different and deeper than the one you lost. It will be something completely new. Everyone has faith of one kind or another—I don't necessarily mean religious faith, I mean the beliefs about ourselves and the world that we each carry, that help us make sense of our lives. This faith is constantly being challenged and renewed. But sometimes it is shattered.

When this happened to me I had no idea that I was being blessed. I felt lost. I went to see a psychotherapist who listened patiently while I talked. After three sessions I knew I had to go further than she could come with me. That was when I called my friend Jörgen in Sweden. Together we went deeper than I could have imagined possible. What I found when I entered my inner world took me completely by surprise: there was nothing wrong with me. Life was offering me a chance to let go of old assumptions, to clear away whatever was holding me back and to find myself anew. Only I could do this—no religion or teacher or therapist could show me myself. I was being given the freedom to choose a new way to be.

How was it, I wondered, that I could have been on a spiritual path for forty years, only to find myself beginning all over again, as if from a blank slate? I was not exactly starting from nothing: it was more like coming full circle. I was reminded of T S Elliot's lines in *Little Gidding*:

And the end of all our exploring
Will be to arrive where we started
And know the place for the first time.

That place was my own heart. I had experienced enough to be willing to trust my inner voice. I no longer wanted to look outside myself for answers, I wanted to find that inner voice of wisdom and let myself be guided by my deepest intuition.

This inner journey is never easy. It still requires a regular spiritual practice; meditation in particular helped me find myself all over again. The thing to remember with spiritual practice is that none of us are perfect. We do the best we can. There will be good days when everything comes easily, and there will be days when we can't seem to get anything right. No matter. We keep on doing the best we can, moving toward the great treasure of self-awareness and self-acceptance, and the freedom of a healthy mind.

TRUE CHOICE

Mind has the power to change the world from the inside outwards. No matter what changes we make to our outer world, unless we change our inner world, our state of mind, we will not resolve our problems.

If we change our inner state, then outer change will naturally follow. This is the unique gift of human life: we can direct our thoughts to bring about conscious change; we are not entirely bound by nature to follow pre-ordained patterns of behaviour. We can choose how we wish to be.

True choice emanates from the deepest level of our being. From there choice manifests in the mind, expressing our underlying consciousness in the thoughts we hold and in the ways we express them in our words and deeds. An example of a profound choice that emanates from deep within is the decision to live with gratitude and forgiveness. If we practice holding such intentions we will create powerful positive energies in our lives that will effect change in the world around us. There is an urgent need in the world today for these qualities to become the natural qualities of human society.

The deepest choice we can make is to live in love. Our nature is to be love. Fear is the opposite of love, but it serves love by bringing us to our heart. Emotions such as fear, obsession, desire, depression, grief, wonder and joy— all are part of the journey, all are made to bring us to love—to the essence of what matters inside us. Here at the profound core of our being is the wisdom that brings enlightenment.

This wisdom, called *buddhi*, is the seventh element.

MEDITATION—MIND

Close your eyes and enter your inner space.

Notice how the external world is present within you. You hold an impression of your physical surroundings, and an awareness of the people and events in your life.

See how your mind holds limitless space filled with events and characters, all facets of your inner mental world.

Notice how you can colour these impressions according to whatever mood you choose—dark, fearful and depressing; intense, passionate and exciting; or light, spacious and inspiring. You can choose how to experience your inner reality.

Move your awareness deeper.

Notice that you are observing your mind, exercising your will to influence its mood.

Who is this observer, that is deeper and more powerful than your mind?

Notice that this observer has the capacity to hold your mind with detachment, to observe its moods and yet be apart from them.

Move your awareness still deeper.

Observe that part of you that exercises will, that directs your mind.

Who is this observer, that is deeper and more aware than the will that directs your mind?

Notice that this observer has the capacity to hold your intelligence with neutrality, to recognise its choices and yet stand apart from them. This is separate from your mind and intelligence; this unmoved observer simply watches.

Feel this higher self, hear what it has to tell you, open yourself to the inner guidance and assurance it brings you.

Who is this unmoved oberver, that is deeper ansd more aware than both your mind and your intelligence?

The Seventh Element

WISDOM ❖ *Inspiration*

Nab Scar looms over Rydal Water

I AM SITTING IN THE SHADOW OF NAB SCAR, which climbs steeply from the shores of Rydal Water to a jagged ridge against the sky. Its bare sides, scoured by falling rocks and scree, are skirted with woodland and pastures reaching down to the water's edge. It looms above me dark and mysterious, a colossal presence reflected in still waters. When the sun emerges the mountain shines. But now, overcast skies give the crag a shadowy weight, and a breeze ruffles the darkened surface of the mere, whose depths call me to life's mysteries. Inner and outer worlds unite, one mirroring the other. The towering fell emerges from the depths of a hidden world, outer reality rooted in inner space.

Wisdom moves beneath the surface of the world as the invisible web that connects all. The tiniest creature has its share of knowledge. Insects or ants know innately how to fit into the web of life. A bird knows how to build a nest without having to be taught. This is because of the presence of wisdom. On a grand scale, planets stay in their orbits and regulate the conditions that support life because they have wisdom. The element of wisdom is present throughout the universe as the organising principle. Each particle possesses consciousness, and wherever consciousness is present there also is the guiding principle of wisdom.

Earth is not the only place in the cosmos that supports life. Life manifests in any condition it wishes, since life is not material. The spirit can be present in any of the eight elements or any combination of them. From this perspective we do not need to detect the presence of carbon, hydrogen, oxygen or nitrogen to know that life might be present. We could however say that wisdom, organising intelligence, is a condition for life.

DANCE OF LIFE

We have the capacity to receive the universal wisdom. Just as a radio receiver detects radio waves and converts them to information, so on a more subtle level the wisdom receiver embedded inside us detects the universal consciousness, the mind of God spread throughout space. This receiver is like an unerring compass that points us toward the Source. This is how all life forms, from the smallest to the largest, have the capacity to integrate into ever more complex organisms in the harmonious dance of life. All become a projection of the conscious organising principle that pervades the universe.

I see this inner receiver as a sphere of golden light that shines in the region of my heart; a flame burning in my innermost sanctuary. The region of the heart is often spoken of as the abode of spirit and the place where the divine consciousness touches our own. This is where I feel wisdom present. It is the subtlest of material elements, that allows me to converse with my creator. In this sense my heart is the abode of God.

Inner life is as full of variety as outer life, yet with even more possibilities, because internally we are not bound by the laws of time and space as we are externally. The element of wisdom works together with the mind and senses to create endless varieties of inner experience.

Wisdom manifests in two primary ways: wisdom of the head and wisdom of the heart.

WISDOM OF THE HEAD: INTELLIGENCE

Intelligence inhabits the mind and senses to perceive and understand the world in all its levels of reality. The seat of this perception the inner eye within the brow, sometimes called the third eye. Working through the brain, this perception observes and understand the physical world to scrutinise and question our observations as a way to understanding. Working with the inner senses and intuition, intelligence visualises and gives inspiration, creating endless varieties of internal experience.

Dreams

In dreams my intelligence freed from mental interpretations can manifest pure intuition, and reveal the world in new and inspiring ways. I am sometimes guided like this. In a dream something is said, something happens that makes a deep impression on me. I wake with a clear memory of it, yet although it feels significant it rarely makes immediate sense. I have learned that if I wait a day or two and allow my mind to absorb the dream and integrate its parts, a message reveals itself.

For example, not long ago I had a vivid dream in which I saw myself in a company of beautiful people, all waiting our turn to receive gifts. A voice kept repeating, 'don't stop me.' Then I was beside a swollen river, a glistening rising flood dangerous for some but not for me, because I was shown the way to higher ground. I was led to a jetty from where I was to embark on a journey. At this moment I awoke from my dream.

What did the dream mean? I had no idea, but I noted it in my journal. Weeks later I understood the dream as a message of encouragement and assurance, telling me that I am on a journey bringing gifts and growth. None of this was apparent to me at the time. The biggest mystery for me was the voice saying, 'don't stop me.' At first I couldn't identify the speaker or what was meant. Then I realised this was the voice of my deeper self telling me not to resist and to let God's will work through me.

What is happening here? First of all, dreams sometimes come from the deeper self, the place of wisdom. Secondly, dreams are rarely apparent straight away – their messages are revealed to the waking consciousness over time. With patience all becomes clear. I find the same is true of waking life.

Life's experiences rarely make much sense as they occur. But if we wait, then over time their significance reveals itself. No event is purely accidental. All is pervaded by cosmic intelligence, harmonised and integrated so that each of us experiences ourself and grows as a part of the whole. Intelligence is apparent in all aspects of life, interior, exterior, waking life and dreams. This is how wisdom speaks to us through the world of experience.

Visions

In states of deep concentration the inner eye opens to the luminous worlds of pure intuition, where the subtle senses bring visions of higher realities. These realities exist in realms we do not normally perceive, that vibrate at higher frequencies than the earthly ones. They belong to the subtle worlds of ether and mind and can only be perceived by the subtle senses. The unseen powers that inhabit these regions have immense influence on our lives. We communicate with them, and they with us, when we are in deeper states of consciousness.

Such visionary experiences when they come are a great blessing. The symptom of this inner vision is the presence of light. This is because the inner realms are luminous. They have their own inner light. The experience of seeing them is one of actually seeing another reality—a vision as different from imaginary vision as actually meeting and conversing with a person is from thinking of meeting that person.

Perception of these inner realities is not limited to sight; they may also be perceived through sound, touch, smell or pure cognition. All these perceptions are subjective; real to the perceiver but not to anyone else. Adopting another person's intuitive experiences as if they are objective truth can be misleading, yet this is common practice in religious traditions, in which one individual's inspiration can become the basis for beliefs that over time become far removed from the original vision.

At the beginning of this book I described the vision that inspired me to write. That experience was more real to me than waking life, yet I cannot make it real for anyone else. I share it in the hope it will confirm other people's own intuitions. In the end we all receive our intuition and inspiration from the same source.

We learn from inspired voices of wisdom and experience, trusting them as our instincts tell us to; we learn from living teachers; from saints and mystics of the past; from books of wisdom; from friends; from everyone we meet and all that we experience. When our experiences and teachers combine with the inner voice of the heart we find wisdom.

The voice inside the heart is our ultimate teacher. If we trust that inner voice then we can trust other voices. If we cannot trust our own self, who can we truly trust? All channels of wisdom coming through the outer world of the senses and the inner worlds of the mind and psychic perception eventually lead to the wisdom that is always with us, the wisdom of the heart.

WISDOM OF THE HEART

This is the deeper manifestation of wisdom. It is memory in the higher sense of remembering divine wisdom. The seat of this wisdom is the region of the heart.

To remember means to reconnect the parts. Remembering is integrating what is already known at a deeper level. The soul holds prior knowledge, from previous experiences in other realms, or as wisdom implanted in seed form by the Creator. When we enter this world we forget this ancient soul wisdom. This forgetfulness is necessary, because without forgetting our higher identity we would not be able to function in a world which demands that we struggle to sustain physical life and live within the limitations of the five senses. My task here is to remember who I am, and in so doing know myself more deeply. The way this ancient memory is introduced to the conscious self is through the higher intelligence, called *buddhi*. This memory is part of the inheritance of each of us, waiting to be discovered or remembered, integrated into our conscious awareness. It is the wisdom we were born with, but which takes time to manifest in our lives.

NATURAL WISDOM

When I was a child I had visions of a larger reality, daydreams in which I explored space and time, trying to understand myself and God, wondering what my life was all about. I used to sit in the garden under an apple tree, and from there I journeyed into the universe seeking an explanation. I felt the presence of divine consciousness and felt

God spread everywhere. I had thoughts I couldn't put into words; when I tried to explain them I was misunderstood by grown-ups. Mostly I kept my experiences to myself. I developed an inner life, which is one of the reasons I liked to walk on my own in the woods, where I could tune into nature undisturbed. As I grew older I forgot a lot of this. My childhood experiences were too difficult for me to understand, so I let them lie. As life crowded around me, with its joys and sorrows, I forgot my visions until they reawakened years later. Perhaps many of us have this experience. We begin life with an inner awareness, a natural wisdom; then we put this wisdom aside to join society, to mix with family, friends and the world.

Our journey through this world spans many lifetimes. It takes time to integrate the wisdom that has been given to each one of us. We are each on our own magical journey, no two alike. Where I am at this moment is the right place for me to be. There is no need for me to compare my wisdom with another's. I have only to be present here and now, to accept and experience whatever I have been given in this moment and at this place. All is given at the right time.

When I am ready to deepen my understanding and remember more about my true purpose, I will be given the means to clear my mind and access my inner wisdom. This will be made easier with spiritual practice. A teacher—guru, guide or mentor—can help me find my path to wisdom, but a teacher cannot find wisdom for me. Hearing from a person whose inner wisdom is awakened has the affect of awakening my own wisdom. The teacher's role is to remind me of what I already know, to awaken my inner ear so that I can hear my own inner voice of divine wisdom.

Now we are living in a time when inner vision is required. We are called upon to remember secrets of the heart, to bring them into our waking lives and share our natural wisdom—a wisdom that belongs to everyone.

RECOGNISING THE AUTHENTIC VOICE

How do we distinguish between the inner voice of wisdom and the whimsical voice of the mind? Can we be misled by trusting our own ideas of truth?

The voice of wisdom is different from the inventions of the mind. The commentary of the mind comes and goes like a babbling brook or the ceaseless wind and can be observed in just the same way: as part of the landscape of life. If I allow its murmurings to pass without resistance they fall silent of their own accord; only if I attend to them do they remain strong.

Yoga postures, meditation, prayer and spiritual reading quiet the mind. So does a walk in nature. A deep satisfaction comes from these practices, filling the mind with peace. As this peace grows, the mind wants to return to it, and so the mind becomes a friend, no longer pulling me away from my spiritual purpose. In the meantime, think of the mind's chatter as you would the ceaseless chatter of a child, or ripples on the surface of a lake. With practice you will hear a deeper voice, an underwater current that flows silently in the depths of the lake. This is the voice of wisdom.

You can recognise the difference between inventions of the mind and messages of deep wisdom with the help of intuition. As you become familiar with your inner life and learn to attend to it, so it will guide you. Each of us has an inner landscape that gives meaning to the one outside. The inner and outer are connected—one would not be real without the other. We would find no meaning in sun or mountain, in tree or animal, in friend or mother, unless we had the inner vision to identify these; the inner awareness of their existence makes them real. In the dream world we have experiences that, when we later remember them, are indistinguishable from memories of waking life. This is because the inner landscape is the essential reality that allows us to make sense of the outer world. With practice you can explore your inner geography to locate your emotions and your wisdom.

THE INNER LANDSCAPE

On the spiritual path all aspects of ourselves—body, mind and spirit—need to be included. Wisdom is not only in the head and heart, it pervades every cell of our body. Consequently, awareness of the whole inner landscape is essential to living with authenticity.

Feelings are our guide to help us recognise authenticity in ourselves and others. Reason is not enough—we have the capacity to experience the world energetically through the body's seven life centres. These energetic centres, called chakras, are the channels through which energy flows to give life to our whole organism. Using the seven chakras as a guide, here is an outline of the inner landscape.

Each of us will feel and locate these chakras in our own way, with our own sensations, colours and sounds. My experience may not correspond precisely with yours, or with what you have heard from others, because we are all different. When the time is right we discover these things for ourselves. This is one person's journey through the inner landscape. I give each chakra a corresponding element and suggest how it helps me discern truth and authenticity.

Root chakra: Earth
Here I receive Earth's living energies and find my stability, self-acceptance and security. Here live my instincts for

survival and self-protection. Here too I hold on to negative emotions such as aversion, disdain, hatred or bitterness.

Here I feel the presence of danger and know where to put my trust.

Sacral chakra: Water

Desires and longings, sexuality and sexual emotions live here, along with their negative connotations of greed, desire for control and possessiveness. Here my creative energy is expressed in dance, music, art, joy and passion; where I can let myself go, have fun and enjoy the excitement of being alive.

Here I am alert to the energy of control and possessiveness, and here I tune into healing energies that nourish me.

Solar chakra: Fire

At the middle of my body is my visceral sense of presence. From here I project the power I receive from nature. It is the home of courage, determination, confidence, ambition and the will to succeed. Here I experience physical fear—the fear that is mixed with pride and anger. Here too I can overcome my fear and let go of my anger.

Here I sense weakness and feel the presence of authentic power.

Heart chakra: Air

The seat of positive loving emotions is the heart chakra. Affection, compassion, empathy, love and attachment live here, as does joy. Yet this is also where I hold emotional fear—that is mixed with sorrow.

Fear and love are closely related: fear holds my heart captive and shuts in love. The feeling of fear is the effort of shielding my heart and holding it closed. At its core is my fear of love. Love invites me to open my heart, to reveal myself, to drop the armour I have built around my innocence. To open my heart can seem a frightening prospect: will I be hurt again? Fear of love leads me to loneliness and sadness.

If I learn to trust, I will find the confidence to release this defensiveness and open my heart. Once I let go of fear and open my heart I feel the love that moves through it, both in giving and receiving, and I experience the natural flow of love that brings emotional well-being and heals all.

Here, when my heart is open I can discern true friendship from false; feel the difference between a relationship of exploitation and one of genuine love.

The inner temple of the heart is the home of my true self. I will return to this inner space at the end of the chakra journey.

Throat chakra: Ether

This is where I experience sensitivity to my surroundings, where self-expression and communication emanate, where my ideas and inspirations become messages to put out into the world. It is the source of song, music and speech. When my throat is open I can broadcast without fear or hesitation, and transmit my positive energy through sound. This chakra is also linked to hearing, to receiving and being sensitive to ideas and inspiration from others. Hearing and speaking are interdependent: conversation in which the power of word is honoured is the foundation of open communication. Hesitation and self-doubt block the throat chakra and hinder free expression. These can be dissolved by hearing and speaking messages expressed with love.

Here I discern honest truth from lies, sincerity from deception; here I tune into uplifting and healing sounds.

Brow chakra: Mind

My brow is the seat of vision, understanding and reason, where I perceive nature, act and react to assert my intentions. Here I hold my self-image and my image of reality. Here is the seat of my sense of duty, justice and obligation. Here also I hold pride and wilfulness. Pride can be dissolved by meditation and contemplation of philosophy.

The brow is the seat of my third eye which brings mystic vision of the higher dimensions.

Here I recognise life-affirming visions and distinguish them from fanciful dreams or ideas based on egotism.

Crown chakra: Wisdom

The crown is the seat of spiritual wisdom. Here lives knowledge that is detached from worldly things, and my awareness of eternity.

Here I distinguish reality from illusion.

Temple of the Heart: Ego

The crown returns me to the inner temple of my heart, the seat of eternal love. Ego, which pervades the chakra system, dwells in its pure form as true self-knowledge in the inner temple of the heart. Here the self encounters the loving presence of God and receives the voice of the Inner Guide. The more I allow the vibration of love to flow in my heart the more I am aware of this divine loving presence.

This inner landscape can be explored as an exercise during meditation. Through repeated journeys you can know your inner world. As inner awareness grows it brings the ability to recognise authentic experience and truth.

The centre of the inner landscape is the heart. To live life from the heart is to be in touch with love. Love is more powerful than any other emotion. It overcomes all barriers and heals all ills. When the mind is suffused with love it becomes like the clear glass of a lamp, allowing wisdom to shine through from the divine source.

Like the dial of a radio, once my heart is tuned to the frequency of love the messages of divine wisdom come through ever clearer. When tuned to love, the mind and all the senses become illuminated. The direct way to this illuminated state is to live in a spirit of service. Service aligns the senses and the eight elements with love so they transparently shine light and wisdom into the world.

SPIRIT OF SERVICE

When we use inspired knowledge to work with the elements of nature, wisdom flows through every part of our being. In this state of awareness, we manifest heaven on earth—each element reveals and reflects the divine presence. Earth can be cultivated to grow nourishing foods in healthy soil, and made into beautiful forms of shelter and celebration; water allowed to flow freely and unpolluted is a source of healing and inspiration; fire serves us to cook and create, to illuminate and inspire our spirit; air cleanses and renews; ether flows to bring healing sounds, vitality and vision into our lives; mind focused on friendship, caring and service is a source of happiness and joy; wisdom applied to the philosophy of the spirit, and to the benefit of the world, brings illumination. Ego, when freed from attachment and prejudice, radiates joy and love.

This is what I mean by a life of service: its essence brings healing and fulfilment to both giver and receiver. An act that benefits only the performer is incomplete; so is an act that benefits only the recipient. True service benefits all. That is how this world is made, for us to thrive by mutual love and service.

The element of wisdom is not itself the source of life. Wisdom alone is not enough. There is a conscious entity who exhibits that wisdom, who expresses it in a conscious way. Life without consciousness would be mere intelligent mechanism. The glory of conscious life is that I have the freedom to choose how to be, how to express my love, compassion and wonder. To receive and exhibit wisdom, I have the capacity to contain it, to manifest it as an individual being in this world of matter. This leads me to the final element, ego.

Meditation—Journey to the Heart

Begin at your root, feel your presence on Earth and your instinct for safety. Absorb this feeling and move upward.

In your sacral area feel your sexual energy and your instinct for creativity. Embrace these and move up.

At your solar centre feel your power and your will to engage with the world. Embrace these and move up.

Enter your heart chakra, feel love and friendship for those who inspire your journey, your connection to the community of life. Embrace these and move up.

At your throat honour your wish to hear and be heard, to send and receive messages of love. Embrace these and move up.

Focus on your brow. Perceive your whole experience of life, the impressions from all your senses. Accept your hopes and fears, attachments and desires——they do not define you. Embrace these and move up.

Ascend to the crown of your head. Be open to your connection with universal wisdom, see the light of eternity. Embrace these and enter the core of your heart.

Here at the core of your being is your source of inspiration and tranquillity, the seat of the realisation of I AM. Be grateful for all that is given. Open yourself to the love that pervades all.

The Eighth Element

EGO ✣ *Acceptance*

My meditation room in the cottage

THREE WEEKS AFTER ENTERING THE SILENCE of this place, I have reached the eighth element. As each day passes my journey deepens. Mornings begin upstairs in my small meditation room. I sit here and receive inspiration for the day's writing. The further I come on this journey, the more mysterious my subject and the more I am guided by intuition. As I was promised, words are given to me, and so I have written on ether, mind and wisdom.

All day yesterday from first light a storm raged throu
the valley. Thunder and lightning rolled past followed
driving rain and gales. Last night the wind howled an
pounded on my window. As dawn approached I we
my meditation space with a cup of hot water and a
The wind was dying down, but the rain continu
light revealed a land drowned in mist and clo
sure the window and door were well fastene
and settled down to meditate, beside me my
pen to record any inspiration I would be g

ILLUSIONS OF ACTION

I wanted to learn about ego, the most elusive of the eight elements. Its Sanskrit name is *ahamkara*, which means 'I do.' The Latin word 'ego' meaning 'I' is close in meaning, but lacks the sense of action implied in *ahamkara*. Another description of the element is 'false ego': the imaginary self that arises when the real self is projected from the eternal reality into this temporary world.

Ego is the aura of the self around which the other elements coalesce; the causal presence that gives them form. It is not the aura of the whole self, but of that part of the eternal self that enters this world. Just as air scatters leaves or carries clouds; so the self imparts life to the natural world.

Actions in this world are the work of nature——all the ego supplies is the impulse to act. Nature then creates the illusion that I am doing something, that I am acting as I wish. Nature gives me the costume I wear. Beyond nature is the unknown hand of destiny——the higher power without which nothing can be accomplished. What I think of as my freedom is an illusion——but do I still have free will?

On my spiritual journey, when I started to question life became aware of my deep self. At the same time I rceived another presence, a power greater than me. I wanted to understand my relationship with that higher power, to know who or what it was, how it affected my life, and how I might affect it. At the root of my enquiry were deep existential questions. What am I? What is my source? Where does the balance lie between my destiny and my freedom to choose?

FREEDOM TO CHOOSE

A life-changing choice arises from deep-seated intention. Friends advised me against taking the path of yoga. This was in 1970, when Hindu spirituality was still met in England with incomprehension. But I followed a deep intuition that I must choose this way, and live for a greater purpose. That choice changed my life.

I am sure it was no accident that I chose as I did; it was the outcome of my life to that point. As a child under the apple tree, as a choirboy at worship, as an art student in love—I had speculated about the nature of my soul and God. One choice followed another. Through a series of choices I was creating my life.

I now see that my deepest intention, the one beneath all others, was to align myself with divine purpose. When I immersed myself in ashram life I felt my sense of purpose unfold from my true centre. I found that the 'I am' of my ego was really 'I am love.' The 'I do' of my ego in this world became 'I serve.' By giving up my imagined freedom I found my true purpose, my real ego and my inner freedom.

Now, sitting in the candlelight of my meditation room forty-two years later, I needed to rediscover that sense of inner purpose, to understand again what lay at the heart of my life and my freedom to choose. My mind was empty save for my silent prayer—let me learn about ego.

Peace reigned in the darkness. I lost track of time. When I opened my eyes I saw that an hour had elapsed, daylight had flooded the room and the rain had softened.

My pen lay idle. I reflected that today I would be given nothing new to write. With closed eyes I offered a prayer of acceptance. Just then a breath of cool air brushed my cheek and a shiver passed up my spine. I felt a presence beside me and was given the urge to take up my pen and paper.

The words that began to flow across my page came not from my mind, nor my imagination, but from a voice of guidance in my heart. I asked questions, and as they were answered I felt a deep inner connection with the same guiding presence that had started me on this journey. I had the conviction that I could put any question and receive an answer. The answers were to be shared in this book. Please take from them whatever speaks to you, and leave aside the rest.

Here is the dialogue that followed.

Thank you for being here with me.

I am always with you. I spread light around you and fill you with hope. I give you wisdom to know what it is you do and why you are here.

Please tell me about the ego.

The true name for this is the ray of the soul.

Each of you is more powerful than you can imagine, because you are an eternal child of God. Just as there is no limit to the glories of the Beloved Creator of All, so there is no limit placed upon his children.

If they want to experience their own life—to play at being creators—he gives them that experience.

If we are unlimited children of God, why do we suffer and experience doubts?

Because you have not yet learned to use your divine nature—you are like a child who wants to be in charge and meets with frustration.

Listen to the guidance in your heart. When you

entered this world you had a clear purpose, a divine purpose. Now your task is to remember that.

Why did I forget?

Forgetfulness is part of the experience. By forgetting and rediscovering you learn again the truth and eternal beauty of who you are.

Your true nature is Love—you are deeply, profoundly, magnificently in love with your Beloved Creator and with all the brilliant creations of your true Beloved.

Then why do I see pain and suffering in this world?

It is the pain of loss, of imagining you are lost and have lost what you can never lose. The pain you see is never ignored—your Creator sends comforting angels to the afflicted. In their pain, in their loss, is true love found.

Who am I in my true state?

While you are here in this world you can never truly know the answer to this question. But I will tell you this. You are full of love, perfectly created as an eternal child of love. Your nature is to love. Your eternal occupation is to share love.

That is what you are here to learn—better to share your love in every possible way.

So what is ahamkara, *false ego?*

It is the reflection of the soul, of you, in this world. Like in a dream—the dream persona.

Because this is your reflection you have not the full glory of your true eternal self.

Remember what Krishna said, 'With a single fragment of myself I pervade and support this entire universe.' You are such a fragment. Yet your true power is hidden. If it were to manifest in full this world would vanish in an instant from your vision. But you do not want that now because you are here to serve a great purpose.

What is that purpose?

It is the unfolding love of the Lord of all Love, who wishes to share his love with all his fragments.

How am I able to help that?

You are directed from within to meet the persons you can benefit, by giving them your comfort, friendship, wisdom and affection—by reflecting a little of His divine love while they journey in the dreamworld to find themselves. Every child of God is special—each one has his or her own journey of light and darkness to make.

All creatures of the Beloved are watched and guided at all times—they need never fear or feel forgotten.

Please tell me how ego is spread through the universe.

Ego is present in all beings, as the sunshine is everywhere of varying intensity because of the clouds. Sometimes the sun burns, it is so bright and strong. Other times it barely illuminates through the thick cloud cover. Some beings are full of clear spirit that is bright enough to illuminate the way for countless others.

How are people misled to create suffering?

The ego is too strong. Darkness overcomes it and it becomes a negative force.

Freedom is an essential part of life here. If there is no freedom, life will lead nowhere.

To learn takes time and repeated experience.

When your heart is open you learn faster.

Tell me about higher beings

Why do you use the word higher? All are glorious.

Some are more connected to the directing from the Divine Source of All. There is no difference between them and God because their only wish is to do God's will.

Tell me about guilt and forgiveness.

The feeling of guilt arises when you take responsibility for the actions of others. You have your own actions which you must take care of—the pain you have caused others inadvertently or intentionally accumulates like sand on the riverbed, until the watercourse is hindered. If the water flows clear it can wash away this pain and the feelings of guilt it brings.

How is guilt caused by feeling responsible for others?

Because only God is responsible. You are trying to play God's role. Each person has their own unbreakable link with God. All matters of guilt, blame, shame and pain are resolved and healed in this inner world. Each of you must attend to your own inner conversation with God, then the water of God's grace flows and washes clean the inner space. When you look to others you do not see your own mistakes and so you succumb to the burden of shame. Remember what Jesus said—first take the log from your own eye before you can remove the splinter from another's.

Chanting God's names is the most powerful cleanser of shame. It washes it away. That is why everyone is uplifted by chanting. When you chant, visualise the presence of God flowing through you, cleansing your heart.

What is the role of forgiveness here?

It is giving attention to your own inner healing—accepting the love and the presence of your Beloved Creator to clear your own burden of shame. Once you are clear and flowing within, you can shine your light and your love. You can become an agent of the Lord to bring that inner cleansing of forgiveness to others.

Why is forgiveness so important?

It is the clearing of the channel of love. Love is the energy that sustains all creation. Creation is made to share love.

✦

GRATITUDE

Remembering these words I feel immense gratitude. I understand that instead of me controlling nature she is controlling me, and I accept her power with an open heart. She is caring for me, feeding me, loving me, healing me, teaching me. If I allow her, she will work wonders through me.

Realising this I see the love in everything. I no longer experience hardship or discomfort as trials to avoid—I accept whatever comes, painful or pleasant, and embrace it as part of life. I no longer need to feel shame or guilt, because I know I am in the care of nature and the Creator, of Goddess and God, as is every other being. The final gift of ego is to be filled with gratitude.

IN THE DARKNESS IS LIGHT

Near the end of writing this book I was shown a great lesson. I experienced excruciating pain when I had an episode of acute retention—that is, I was unable to pass urine. A friend got up in the night and drove me to hospital, where I was drained and fitted with a catheter tube that was removed after a few days. Three weeks later it happened again, only this time it was more difficult: I was camped in a field and the hospital was fifty miles away.

Back at home the following night, weak and bewildered, I drifted in and out of sleep, constantly reminded of the urine bag again strapped to my leg. At first I resisted. Then I heard in my semi-conscious state a soothing voice repeatedly telling me, 'Accept what is happening, be in the spirit.' I felt bathed in love and light, and was made to understand that far from being unfortunate I was being blessed, healed and cleansed on a subtle level to allow me to be more open and to make way for inner growth. All I had to do was let go of my resistance and allow it.

For the next five weeks until the catheter was removed I embraced my condition and felt blessings and love. I was taught that pain does not have to be resisted and fought against—it can be accepted as a blessing. In the darkness is light. In the pain is love.

✦

The messages in this chapter came to me as an unexpected blessing. For three days I was led through the ego by a guiding voice of love. On the fourth day I walked in the clear morning air, following a winding path along the shore of Rydal Water and Grasmere. As the sun broke through the clouds and glistened on the water my heart filled with gratitude. I felt that my journey through the elements had reached its fulfilment.

MEDITATION—GRATITUDE

Remember someone in your life who is special to you. Consider how this person assists and teaches you in your journey. What have you learned from this person? Imagine he or she were no longer here with you. How would you feel? Think of this person with gratitude.

MEDITATION—FORGIVENESS

Think of someone with whom you have experienced conflict. Do you hold any negative emotions toward this person? Is this linked with personal feelings of shame or guilt? Can you allow forgiveness toward yourself and the other person? How does this feel?

Has your interaction taught you something? Can you feel gratitude for the role this person played in your life?

SPIRIT

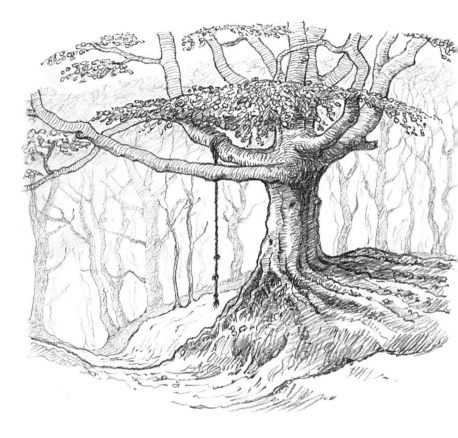

The great beech of the Forest of Dean

NOW I HAVE JOURNEYED THROUGH this world of eight elements, I can look with fresh eyes at what might lie beyond these elements. That transcendental realm beyond is hidden within this one. If I open my inner eye and ear, open my heart, I will find that wondrous realm of love.

To know the eight elements, if I could ever conceive of their vastness, would still be to know only a fraction of all that is. At the place where I know myself, where the 'I do' of my shadow ego becomes the 'I am' of my transparent ego, I move into truth, where my self and my self-expression are one, where there is no difference between essence and form, where I live and act in full conscious awareness.

It was now late autumn. To enter the spirit I needed to find fresh inspiration. I wanted to be in the forest, somewhere I could let my roots sink deep into Mother Nature and my heart rise to the spirit. I went to stay with my friends in the Forest of Dean, a secret place of dreams and songs of nature beside the Severn Estuary. There, as the leaves turned golden, I was led into the forest to a great spreading beech, sentinel of the valley depths. Its high over-hanging boughs, hung with ropes, offered a playground for children. The clay at its feet, filled with crumbling stones, sloped into the valley. This tree symbolised my journey through nature and the rooting of myself into the realm of the Goddess, Mother Earth.

As I contemplated this two hundred-year-old tree, so grounded in earth and stone, an inner space was revealed to me: water covered by mist and swirling vapours; currents of ether; dreams, starlight, the vastness of space filled with life; all suspended in the embrace of the Cosmic Creator.

SEEING MYSELF

I walked on through the forest, seeing around me this world of elements as a hall of mirrors, nothing as it seemed. What appeared as solid matter was etheric space. Yet this elemental world had the magical quality to show me myself. I saw my consciousness reflected back to me in a mirror of infinite facets. I realised how in endless ways, seeing always my face in the face of the world, I learn who I am, who I am not, and who I wish to be. In each person I meet—my brother, my sister, my mother, my lover—I see myself. All show me who I am.

The most moving experience of self this fleeting world

of mirrors has offered me is the experience of falling in love, for in the eyes of my beloved I meet myself. This meeting hints at something great and transcendent. It promises a deeper way of being; a life saturated with love, in which every act is suffused with deep awareness of divine presence, illuminated by a joy that lights up all it touches, and a love that extends to all.

MOMENT

Could I find such intensity of experience in the present moment, whatever it might be? Let me try.

I sit here in the Forest of Dean at a desk and chair made from forest oak. I write with a hand-crafted fountain pen; surrounded by books holding ideas from hundreds of lives and loves distilled into ink on paper bound in card and cloth. On the window sill a candle burns at my votive pictures, signifying the blessings of divine beings here with me.

Outside my window across the Severn Estuary distant blue hills spread beneath an oceanic sky flooded with sunlight and scattered with billowing white clouds. Close at hand clusters of oak and beech conceal stone cottages wrapped in clematis and wisteria. Beneath my window three hundred gravestones sink into the turf of a forest churchyard.

I hear birdsong, the whisper of a passing car, the creak of central heating pipes, a door closing, the scratching of my pen, my hand sliding across the page as I write—I breathe, blood pulses in my ears, I swallow, the clock ticks. No breath of wind disturbs my engulfing peace. This experience is uniquely mine, never to be repeated, my mirror of self given by the Source of All at this moment... and this one... and this one...

I AM NOT ALONE

As I pass through life I experience myself in endless ways; each day the sun rises to show me another facet of myself. If I am deeply blessed and fortunate I become aware that I am not alone. This mirror that shows me myself, this mysterious and wondrous world of matter, also sees me. That which shows me myself also has self, a Self so magnificent as to encompass all other visions of self.

This Self is like the sun. All life depends on the sun. Hence all life loves the sun. If I look upon the sun, as humans have throughout history, as a conscious being of unimaginable power, I see that all life is a love affair between Earth and Sun. Both are within me, Earth the womb and Sun the progenitor.

If God is the source of life and love, Goddess is the one

who is loved and returns that love. She is in all things. The whole realm of nature is She. Yet it is also He. This is the divine mystery; they cannot be separated. Both are in me—the Energy and the Source, She and He, Goddess and God, Lover and Beloved.

UNION OF FEMALE AND MALE

The union of female and male is woven into the foundation of the world. Every being has a mother and a father. When the mother and father unite a child is born. It is so clear, so plain, yet so mysterious.

In our passage through this world we dress sometimes as male, sometimes as female, sometimes as a combination of both. Sometimes I am mother, sometimes father. In each role—female or male—I experience new understandings. We include within us both natures, the feminine and the masculine. This is why we are drawn to one another, because we recognise ourselves in each other.

The integration of the male and female within brings a self-awareness in which both sides of the self find union. A current flows unceasingly through the heart, uniting the twin poles of male and female. God and Goddess exist eternally in the transcendent reality and their union is reflected within me.

LOVER AND BELOVED

Beyond this world of temporary forms is the everlasting Source. My eternal self in relation to the Source of All is both lover and beloved. I am never alone. My dearest and closest Friend knows and loves me through all eternity. I have the possibility to enter an everlasting embrace in my heart. Once inner love is awakened my life becomes an unfolding love affair with the Source Of All, my Friend and Beloved.

This divine love is at the heart of the world's mystical traditions. The Song of Solomon, the love poems of Rumi, Juliana's *Revelations of Divine Love*, the Dark Night of Saint John of the Cross, the prayers of Sri Chaitanya—down through the ages all have spoken of it. In my youth I was given a glimpse of this transcendent love in the mystical dance of Radha and Krishna, and I have served it ever since. My heart tells me that all reality is the play of Their Love.

My meditation today began with a guardian tree, the great beech of the Forest of Dean. Strength and playfulness, the dangling ropes—I saw children playing, reminding me that in the Source of All, playfulness is equal to love.

The Goddess manifests as the spirit of love, as mother to her children, as wisdom, Sophia, Sarasvati, Holy Spirit born of love.

Her love and wisdom appear in the person of the teacher. If you are fortunate to find an authentic spiritual teacher, realise that the teacher is a channel, and don't confuse the channel with the love, grace and wisdom that flow through the channel.

And I am a reflection of the Source of All.

Inside and outside is one. Goddess and God are always and everywhere inside and outside all.

The end is the beginning.

MEDITATION: THE CALL

I call upon sacred names, healers of my soul. I call on the infinite in the universal mantra, Om. I call the names of Goddess and God. Their names are unlimited. I choose the ones that respond to me as I call them.

When I chant, I visualise the names flowing through me, cleansing my heart, knowing there is no difference between inside and outside; that Goddess and God dwell inside and outside all creation: within the atom and in all of space.

In all that I see, as well as in the core of my heart, I find no separation between me and my Divine Source.

CLOSING WORDS

The giant oak, mother tree of Hampstead Heath

IT IS SPRING AGAIN, NEARLY TWO YEARS after I began writing about the elements in the Lakeland cottage. I am in London and have come, as generations of artists and writers have before me, to the peace of Hampstead Heath. Sitting in the roots of a giant oak, I am at the source of the River Fleet, which trickles from beneath this tree through a hidden valley toward the city. On either side, sloping banks thick with oak, birch and holly are deep in last year's fallen leaves.

The sun's rays, gaining in warmth after the spring equinox, thicken buds and open blossoms. Mighty branches curl above me into the air. On one of them a robin warms himself, his red breast brightened by a ray of spring sunshine. A finch pours down a waterfall of high-pitched song. A blackbird swoops low over the undergrowth.

This ancient resident of the forest, whose roots are thrust deep into the earth, has stood here for at least three hundred years. An amphitheatre of great trees grow around it. They echo with the song of countless birds sending up a chorus of adoration for the Creator. I am in nature's cathedral.

Overhead, planes circle on their way to Heathrow, but close at hand I am wrapped in the timeless sounds of the forest and the presence of these trees that reach into the ether, fixing themselves in the fabric of space and filling it with their conscious presence.

I am grateful that this sheltered spot survives in the midst of a vast city. It survives because it is loved, because generations of people have come here to walk with their dogs, to picnic with their children, to nourish their minds and hearts, to compose poetry. We are part of these woods and they are part of us. They restore our spirits. This is why the woods will always survive. When all else is burned away the woods will return.

If you have come with me this far, I am grateful to you. I hope the journey has enriched you as it has me. I began in a state of disintegration, afloat in endless emptiness. For nearly two years my life stood still. In time I was sent messengers, helpers, guides, I was put on my feet and inspired to explore the elements of nature. I discovered far beyond my expectations. I was blessed a thousand times. My spirit was revived: I found again the place where I began, yet deeper and more magnificent, a place of inner light and wisdom. The adventure continues. There will be more challenges, more lessons, more gifts. And I know I will never be alone. Always more. Greater love, greater joy.

From a cloth bag I take my string of beads. A hundred and eight pieces of sacred wood polished smooth and round. As each bead passes through my fingers I murmur my mantra, holding the vibration in my heart. The beads glow warm and golden. The stream flows ever onward.

Hare
Goddess, Mother of Love

Rama
Source of All, Inner Guide

Hare
Fount of Mercy, Who Serves All

Krishna
Enchanter,
Who Manifests in the Heart
of the One Who Loves

Om

Shanti—peace in the self
Shanti—peace on Earth
Shanti—peace in the heavens

INDEX